Law and Society
Recent Scholarship

Edited by Melvin I. Urofsky

A Series from LFB Scholarly

Student First Amendment Speech and Expression Rights
Armbands to Bong HiTS

R. Chace Ramey

LFB Scholarly Publishing LLC
El Paso 2011

Library of Congress Cataloging-in-Publication Data

Ramey, R. Chace, 1978-
   Student First Amendment speech and expression rights : armbands to
bong hits / R. Chace Ramey.
      p. cm. -- (Law & society : recent scholarship)
   Includes bibliographical references and index.
   ISBN 978-1-59332-473-5 (hardcover : alk. paper)
   1. Freedom of expression--United States. 2. Students--Legal status,
laws, etc.--United States. I. Title.
   KF4770.R36 2011
   342.7308'5--dc23
                                                    2011021133

ISBN 978-1-59332-473-5

Printed on acid-free 250-year-life paper.

Manufactured in the United States of America.

For Granddad,
who taught me more than any book
or class ever could

Table of Contents

PART I

Opening the School House Gates

In Des Moines, Iowa, a group of students wore black armbands to school to protest the United States involvement in the Vietnam War. Across the country, in Juneau, Alaska, students displayed a banner stating "BONG HiTS 4 JESUS" for television cameras as the Olympic torched passed in front of their school. Although separated by nearly 3,000 miles and taking place 40 years apart, the students in each circumstance claimed that their actions were forms of constitutionally protected student expression. In each instance, school leaders suppressed the expression and disciplined the students for exhibiting the behavior. Unlike countless other clashes between students and public school leaders over student expression, the results of these situations were not determined by the school administration or even the local school board. The United States Supreme Court passed final judgment on the constitutionality of both forms of these students' expression.

In *Tinker v. Des Moines Indep. Sch. Dist.* (1969), the United States Supreme Court reached resolution regarding the constitutionality of the students' black armband protest. The Court's decision constituted its first substantial impact on student expression in school, and radically changed students' abilities to exercise their speech or expression rights under the First Amendment to the U.S. Constitution.[1] In writing his majority opinion in *Tinker*, Justice Fortas

---

[1] Student speech and/or expression encompasses student speech; student press; student verbal and non-verbal expressive actions; distribution of petitions; literature and flyers; cyber communication including internet blogs, social

penned, "It can hardly be argued that either students or teachers shed their constitutional rights to freedom of speech or expression at the schoolhouse gate" (*Tinker*, p. 506). The decision, and this specific statement, established that students do not automatically forfeit all freedoms simply because they enter public school. The statement also supported the *Tinker* Court's ultimate finding that the students' black armband protest was protected expression under the First Amendment to the U.S. Constitution.

Thirty-eight years after the Court handed down the *Tinker* decision, Chief Justice Roberts quoted Justice Fortas' often cited statement in the Court's most recent student expression decision. The Chief Justice made the statement the starting point of his majority opinion in *Morse v. Frederick* (2007). Unlike Justice Fortas' majority in *Tinker*, Chief Justice Roberts' *Morse* majority found that the student expression at issue was not constitutionally protected. The Supreme Court concluded that the students' "BONG HiTS 4 JESUS" banner was not protected student expression and that school officials could limit such student expression at school activities (p. 2629).

The transition to limiting students' speech and expression rights in schools began almost immediately following the creation of the student speech rights. After elegantly stating that students do not shed their rights when they enter school, Justice Fortas concluded that student speech and expression:

> ... in class or out of it, which for any reason -- whether it stems from time, place, or type of behavior -- materially disrupts class work or involves substantial disorder or invasion of the rights of others is, of course, not immunized by the constitutional guarantee of freedom of speech. (*Tinker*, p. 513)

The statement complicated the student speech and expression analysis because it established that students' freedoms are not unlimited and that certain circumstances exist that allow school leaders to suppress student speech and expression. Furthermore, the

---

networking profiles, email, instant messenger and texting; participation in saluting the flag; and expression through student attire.

finding did not specifically articulate which student speech and expression that was unconstitutional; rather, the Court offered that it was the effect of the speech – the materially disruption of class work – that dictated the constitutionality of the expression. However, the Court left it to school leaders to try and decipher, in specific circumstances what expression creates a substantial material disruption.

Morse was not the first time that the Supreme Court parted ways with the logic put forth in *Tinker*. In the 40 years since *Tinker*, the Supreme Court has decided two additional cases specifically concerning student expression in public schools: *Bethel Sch. Dist.* v. *Fraser* (1986), and *Hazelwood Sch. Dist.* v. *Kuhlmeier* (1988). In *Fraser*, the Supreme Court provided that students' rights in school are not the same as adults in other facets of society (*Fraser*, p. 682; *Morse,* p. 2622). The deconstruction of *Tinker* continued in *Kuhlmeier* when the Court stated that students' rights must be evaluated in light of the special characteristics of the school environment (*Kuhlmeier*, p. 266; *Morse* p. 2622). *Morse* reiterated these additional considerations for analyzing student speech and expression rights in school, expressed that there was more than one approach to analyzing the constitutionality of student expression in school, and added that schools could suppress certain types of speech, specifically student speech that encouraged illegal drug use (*see Morse*, p. 2627) in school or at school related events.

The effect of the four decisions has been a fragmented approach to defining the legal boundaries of student speech and expression in school. The Supreme Court's guidance has left school leaders struggling to understand and apply the Court's decisions in a consistent manner when confronted with student speech and expression dilemmas. This is demonstrated by the stream of student speech and expression disputes that continue to find their way into courtrooms because of disagreement over the constitutionality of the student speech and expression. *Tinker* provided a starting point for student speech and expression rights in school, but 40 years after that decision the Supreme Court's approach and the exact extent of students' constitutional speech and expression rights in school remains unclear.

The federal courts have developed an extensive record of involvement in determining the proper scope of student speech and expression in schools. Protest armbands and pro-drug banners have been joined by school campaign condoms, religious candy canes, parody principal MySpace pages, drug and sex laced Facebook postings and pictures, sexual innuendo filled school election speeches, ill-advised student newspaper articles, and drug and religious charged band music as student speech and expression issues that have been decided in the courtroom rather than the principal's office. Although the federal courts have undoubtedly stated that it is primarily the role of the school to educate students, the federal courts have played a major part in determining the extent to which students may exercise the constitutional rights they learn about in class while still in school or participating in school-sponsored events.

America's schools are becoming forums where students unabashedly attempt to exercise what they believe are their constitutional rights, leaving teachers and administrators to determine whether the student conduct is constitutionally protected or exceeds these protections and falls within the purview of school control. However, drawing a clear distinction between constitutional student speech and expression and student speech and expression that falls outside the protection of the First Amendment to the U.S. Constitution has become more complex. Student expression has expanded from verbal speech in the classroom, hallways, lunchroom, and written expression in school newspapers, underground newspapers, and written flyers to include in-school video communication, web postings, online blogs and chats, social networking profiles, and cell phone text communications. At the same time that the forms of student expression are expanding, an increased concern over school violence and school safety, and a renewed focus on student academic success under the federal No Child Left Behind Act, has spread across the nation. The combination of these competing interests places school leaders in the difficult position of maintaining safe and secure schools focused on academic success while respecting the constitutional speech and expression rights student retain even after they enter through the "schoolhouse gates".

The student speech and expression rights landscape has been broadly defined by the Supreme Court in its four student expression decisions. However, these four decisions do not address every potential situation or type of student expression that might be exhibited, and they do not provide clear guidance when school leaders are faced with competing interests. Student speech and expression that does not specifically align with an articulated First Amendment right forces school leaders to speculate about how much control they may exert to maintain a constructive learning environment. The extent of students' constitutionally protected rights, and where limitations actually begin in relation to the annunciated rights, remains unclear. Lower federal court decisions, which apply the parameters of student speech and expression expressed by the Supreme Court, must be reviewed, analyzed, and interpreted to benefit school leaders. This is necessary so that education leaders may gain a greater comprehension of the limits of protected student rights.

This is the focus of this book – wade through the confusion and bring a degree of clarity to the murky realm of what actually constitutes protected student speech in school. School leaders should gain a better understanding what should be considered when determining whether students have exceeded their protected rights or whether a proposed limitation on student expression is valid. A review and analysis of the current legal framework of student expression rights in school provides valuable information that will assist education leaders in making informed decisions, rather than assumptions, regarding student speech and expression.

Included in the following chapters is a review the current legal boundaries of student speech and expression rights in school, as developed and defined by the U.S. federal courts. The purpose of discussing these decisions is to better enable educators to make informed decisions regarding student speech and expression when confronted with such situations. Federal court student speech and expression decisions published between January 1, 1983 and November 1, 2010 were examined.[2] Special attention was paid to reviewing and analyzing the Supreme Court's student speech and expression principles and the lower federal courts' application of these principles

---

[2] *Tinker* (1969) was also examined, which constitutes the only decision analyzed that was published outside the aforementioned timeframe. *Tinker* is included because it represents the Supreme Court's first major decision regarding student expression in school and is crucial to a full discussion of student expression rights.

to a variety of circumstances involving student speech and expression rights.

This book is meant to serve as a useful tool to for addressing circumstances requiring decisions about student speech and expression in school. It is designed to emphasize the challenges administrators face in establishing, interpreting, and enforcing the limits of student speech and expression. It provides beneficial information for school leaders concerning the Supreme Court's and lower federal courts' development of student speech and expression rights in public school, and can assist educators in defining the extent of students' current speech and expression rights in school and the proper limits to these rights under the First Amendment to the U.S. Constitution. Educators can use the information to differentiate between constitutional student speech and expression that ignores or exceeds constitutional protections.

The Courts

Decisions regarding student speech and expression in school have been heard in various judicial forums, both at the state and federal level. Because of the variance in state laws, the federal court provides the limited stage for discussing student speech and expression decisions.[3] The federal court system is composed of three basic levels. The United States Supreme Court constitutes the highest court in the land.[4] Nine Justices make up the Supreme Court, and this court's decisions are considered precedent[5] and may only be overruled by later rulings of the Supreme Court or by an action of Congress (*Patterson v. McLean Credit Union*,[6] 1989; *Payne v. Tenn.*,

---

[3] State courts do hear cases involving student speech rights in school; however, these cases are not included in this discussion.

[4] The Supreme Court is also properly referred to as the Court, and will be referenced in this manner at points.

[5] Precedent is defined as a decision that "furnishes a basis for determining later cases involving similar facts or issues" (Black's Law, 2004).

[6] Although the main holding of *Patterson* was later superseded by statute, the Supreme Court explained the importance of adhering to the doctrine of *stare decisis*, and stated that although prior decisions are "not sacrosanct," departure

1991).[7] Federal courts of appeals and district courts are under the jurisdiction of the Supreme Court and must adhere to the doctrine of *stare decisis* regarding Supreme Court decisions (*Tenet v. Doe*, 2005).[8] Although the Supreme Court has original jurisdiction in limited circumstances (*Sosa v. Alvarez-Machain*, 2004),[9] the vast majority of the cases heard by the Supreme Court originate at the district court level. If one or more parties to a law suit are dissatisfied with the result at the district level, the case may be appealed to the appropriate United States court of appeals. After review and ruling by the appropriate court of appeals, a dissatisfied party may make application to have the case heard by the Supreme Court.

---

from the "doctrine of *stare decisis* demands special justification" (*Patterson*, p. 172). The Court went on to point out that Congress has the ability to alter what the Court has done (p. 173).

[7] In affirming the Tennessee Supreme Court's upholding of a defendant's death sentence, the Supreme Court overruled two of its previous decisions and held that evidence related to a victim and the impact of the death on the victim's family was admissible in the sentencing phase of a capital murder proceeding. In discussing its decision to break from its prior holdings, the Court explained the importance of *stare decisis*, and stated that following precedent "is the preferred course because it promotes the evenhanded, predictable, and consistent development of legal principles, fosters reliance on judicial decisions, and contributes to the actual and perceived integrity of the judicial process" (*Payne*, p. 827). However, the Court reasoned that when "governing decisions are unworkable or are badly reasoned," the Court is not bound to follow precedent, and that this is "particularly true in constitutional cases" (p. 828).

[8] In *Tenet*, a case involving a former espionage agent who claimed that the United States failed to provide promised financial assistance to the agent, the Supreme Court discussed the court of appeal's responsibility to follow precedent: "the Court of Appeals should follow the case which directly controls, leaving to this Court the prerogative of overruling its own decisions" (*Tenet*, pp. 10-11).

[9] Although somewhat an ancillary issue, the Court articulated that the Constitution vested the Supreme Court with original jurisdiction over certain matters including cases affecting ambassadors and suits brought by diplomats.

United States Courts of Appeals are the intermediate courts in the federal judicial system, which serve as the appellate court between federal district courts and the U.S. Supreme Court. A court of appeals hears cases that originate in the district courts within its legislatively defined geographical boundaries. There are currently 13 courts of appeals, and these courts are bound by the decisions of the Supreme Court, and previous decisions of that particular court of appeals are considered precedent (*Tenet*, pp. 10-11; *Flagship Marine Servs. v. Belcher Towing Co.*, 11th Cir. 1994).[10] Although a court of appeals can look to the decisions of other courts for guidance, a court of appeals is not bound by the decisions handed down in other jurisdictions.

District courts are located in every state and territory in the Nation. Nearly all federal cases begin at the district court level, and the district court is the level at which trials and fact finding take place. Each State has at least one U.S. district court. These differing levels of decision making have added to the disjointed nature of the student speech framework (much like with any legal issue). District courts within the same court of appeals circuit very well could reach different conclusions on the same issue. Likewise, two courts of appeals could take extremely diverse views of similar legal circumstances.

This variance of opinion adds richness to the American judiciary system but also reveals the importance of placing an emphasis on the decisions of the United States Supreme Court. Under the circumstances addressed here, the focus is specifically on Supreme Court decisions concerning student speech and expression rights in school, and then lower federal court decisions rendered between January 1, 1983, and November 1, 2010, that focused on student speech and expression rights in school under the First Amendment to the U.S. Constitution.

Schools, Students and 1st Amendment Speech

While the nation is dotted with diverse and ever changing school systems, the examined decisions all originated as disputes that began

---

[10] The Eleventh Circuit Court of Appeals stated that prior panel decisions become the law of the circuit and are viewed as circuit precedent.

at a *public* elementary school, middle school, junior high school, senior high, or high school. The main players in these judicial dramas are the nations' children that are enrolled in a public school in grades kindergarten through twelfth grade and the teachers and administrators that have been entrusted with teaching these students to levels of deep understanding and guiding them towards graduation. At issue is the proper extent of student speech and expressive conduct adjudicated to be protected under the First Amendment to the U.S. Constitution.

CHAPTER 1.

Wearing Tinker's Armband

Forty years after it was established that students' rights do not end at the school house gates, school administrators are often left wondering what, if any, ability they have to limit students' speech rights in school. Can a student pass out anti-abortion literature while preaching about the sins of the practice at the lunch room table? Can a 1st grader provide "holiday" treats to her classmates, with a message about the birth of Christ attached? And, is *Rent* an acceptable production for the school's spring musical? Prior to 1969, the answer to all of these questions was most likely – no. Since 1969, an array of student, and conflicting school official, opinions have emerged regarding just how appropriate some of these types of speech and expression may be in the school environment. The decision that started schools, administrators, students and courts down this path: *Tinker v. Des Moines Indep. Sch. Dist.* (1969).

In December 1965, after meeting with family and community members, several students decided to wear black armbands to school to protest the Vietnam War. The school administration learned of the planned student action and adopted a policy, which mandated that any student wearing an armband would be asked to remove it. If any student refused, he or she would be sent home, suspended, and not allowed to return until the student returned without the armband. John Tinker, his sister and one other student wore their armbands to school and were advised that day of the new school regulation. They were sent home and suspended until they agreed to return without them (*Tinker*, p. 504).

Tinker filed suit in the U.S. District Court for the Southern District of Iowa claiming a violation of his First Amendment freedom of expression. The district court upheld the school district's action as reasonable to prevent disruption of the education process. An evenly split Eighth Circuit Court resulted in the district court opinion being affirmed.

In *Tinker* v. *Des Moines Indep. Sch. Dist.*, the Supreme Court addressed a conflict between students' First Amendment expression rights and school leaders' ability to maintain the educational process. The Court's opinion focused on determining the extent of students' speech and expression rights while in school. The Court began with the proposition that the armband demonstration "was closely akin to 'pure speech' which…is entitled to comprehensive protection under the First Amendment" (pp. 504-506). This preliminary conclusion was used as a springboard by the Court to extensively discuss the state of students' constitutional rights in school, specifically students' speech rights.

At the time the, Court was engaging in a discussion that had predominantly been avoided by courts across the country; however, the result was a watershed ideal. A conclusion that has since been articulated in nearly every student rights decision since *Tinker*:

> First Amendment rights, applied in light of the special characteristics of the school environment, are available to teachers and students. *It can hardly be argued that either students or teachers shed their constitutional rights to freedom of speech or expression at the schoolhouse gate.* This has been the unmistakable holding of this Court for almost 50 years. (p. 506, emphasis added)

Thus, the Court began from the position that John Tinker (and all school children) possess rights under the U.S. Constitution, and that these rights must be respected by school leaders. Since the *Tinker* decision, the idea that students do not shed their constitutional rights at the schoolhouse gates has been broadened from encompassing only speech and expression to including privacy, limited search, due process and religious rights (e.g., *Board of Educ.* v. *Earls*, 2002, p. 844). However, the special characteristics of the school environment idea, embedded in the *Tinker* Court's statement, has since been utilized by the Court to counterbalance these constitutional freedoms and justify reduced levels of students' rights in school (*Tinker*, p. 506; *see also New Jersey* v. *T.L.O.*, 1985, p. 348; *Hazelwood Sch. Dist.* v. *Kuhlmeier*, p. 266).

In reinforcing the idea of students' constitutional rights in school, the Court found that teachers and school leaders do not have absolute authority over students (*Tinker*, p. 511), and whether in or out of school, students are considered people under the Constitution. "In the absence of a specific showing of constitutionally valid reasons to regulate their speech, students are entitled to freedom of expression of their views" (p. 511). The *Tinker* Court stated that students' rights do not merely exist in the classroom, but are also present in the cafeteria, on the playing field, and in other places on the school's campus. Further, under *Tinker*, a student may express his or her views, even if controversial, in any of these locations as long as they are expressed without "materially and substantially interfering with the requirements of appropriate discipline in the operation of the school" and without trampling other students' rights (p. 513).

The Supreme Court stated that the challenge of the case was addressing a situation where the exercising of student free expression rights collided with school rules and authority (*Tinker,* p. 508). The Court specifically articulated when it believed that the state or school district could regulate speech:

> In order for...school officials to justify prohibition of a particular expression of opinion, it must be able to show that its action was caused by something more than a mere desire to avoid the discomfort and unpleasantness that always accompany an unpopular viewpoint. Certainly where there is no finding and no showing that engaging in the forbidden conduct would materially and substantially interfere with the requirements of appropriate discipline in the operation of the school, the prohibition cannot be sustained. (p. 509)

The Court found that the students wearing armbands did not provide any reason for school authorities to believe it would cause disruption, materially interfere with the education process, or impinge on other students' rights (p. 509).

> School officials banned...silent, passive expression of opinion, unaccompanied by any disorder or disturbance on the part of petitioners. There is here no evidence whatever of

petitioners' interference, actual or nascent, with the school's work or of collision with the rights of other students to be secure and to be left alone. (p. 508)

Instead, the Court found the school officials' actions were based on a desire to avoid any controversy that might arise because of certain students' expression of opposition to the nation's participation in Vietnam. Further, the Court found that the position taken by the school district constituted viewpoint discrimination because the school had not prohibited the wearing of other political symbols. The ban was not based on an actual disruption or the reasonable forecast of a substantial and material disruption. Thus, school officials prohibiting the wearing of black armbands as a political expression was unconstitutional (p. 511).

Through this decision, the Court established that students retain constitutional rights while at school and specifically have First Amendment speech and expression rights. However, the Court did not go so far as to state that students enjoyed unlimited speech rights. In his dissent, Justice Black adamantly voiced:

> One does not need to be a prophet or the son of a prophet to know that after the Court's holding...some students...will be ready, able and willing to defy their teachers on practically all orders...It is nothing but wishful thinking to imagine that young, immature students will not soon believe it is their right to control the schools. (p. 525)

As a result of the position taken by Justice Black, the majority repeatedly stated that students' First Amendment rights were not without limit.

The Court did not grant students unlimited free speech. Instead, it provided parameters for the proper exercise of the rights, while also noting that the students had affirmative obligations to the State that must be respected and exhibited while at school (p. 511). *Tinker* established that private passive student expression did not offend the Constitution, was protected by the First Amendment, and that students had the right to express this type of speech on school grounds during the school day. However, the decision also articulated that students have the responsibility to exercise their free speech rights in a way that does not materially or substantially disrupt the educational process or invade the rights of others (p. 513). The Court's conclusion in *Tinker* established the first principle for evaluating student speech and expression in school: **Students may voice private political expression, and school leaders may only limit the expression if it substantially and materially disrupts the educational process or invades the rights of other students.** The *Tinker* decision ushered in a new era of Court involvement with student rights and responsibilities in schools. *Tinker* specifically addressed students' speech and expression rights; however, the mandates of *Tinker* concerning students' constitutional freedoms have transcended all areas of student rights, and the *Tinker* rationale has been used in the context of privacy, search, and religion. Although the Court has moved away from the *Tinker* standard in certain circumstances or created exceptions that threaten to swallow the rule, *Tinker* continues to be viewed as the foundation for students' rights in school (see *Morse* v. *Frederick*, Justice Thomas concurrence, p. 2636).

For 17 years, *Tinker* was the only Supreme Court decision concerning student expression in schools. Prior to the Court revisiting student expression in *Fraser* in 1986, research and evaluation of student speech and expression in schools focused on the material substantial disruption standard announced in *Tinker* and its application to a variety of factual situations. However, scholars also began to predict that the Supreme Court's involvement in student speech issues was only beginning.

Tinker was utilized as reinforcing the idea that the role of the school was as a place to inculcate students with certain values rather than a marketplace of ideas subject to student choice. (Freeman, 1984, p. 42). Freeman saw *Tinker* as providing a way to "reconcile the inculcative function served by public education with First Amendment limitations on governmental authority" (p. 3). Freeman pointed out that students do not have an unfettered right to access information or voice opinion, while school leaders have nearly unlimited discretion to determine the general curriculum and to determine the content of courses. The manner in which a teacher conducts a class dictates that he or she make numerous decisions about content and the restriction of some ideas and beliefs. Furthermore, class discussion must be guided and limited to keep on topic and maintain proper classroom decorum. Freeman argued that this was the only way public education could effectively meet educational goals and inculcative objectives (p. 47), and utilize the Court's analysis in *Tinker* as supporting this approach to public education in America.

Freeman also argued that the nature of school did not allow students to simply reject ideas; rather, students could be compelled to read, study, and even learn the values of the school and community (p. 48). Further, he offered that time constraints on the school day and limited educational time dictated that decisions regarding educational content be made, and that school leaders were in the best position to make these decisions. Freeman argued that if school really offered students true access to ideas and information, students would end up dictating the curriculum and how educational time was spent (p. 48). He concluded that this would impair the inculcative duty and nature of school and result in an environment that restricted actual learning. While subsequent Supreme Court decisions would limit the extent of student expression rights originally granted in *Tinker*, Freeman's approach went further in limiting students' freedoms than the Court's subsequent decisions.

In 1981, the Third Circuit Court of Appeals published a decision upholding a superintendent's ability to censor a school played based on his belief that the play was inappropriate. Faaborg (1985) took exception to the court's ruling and published an article that was highly critical of the decision calling it superficial as well as incorrect, and the conclusions relied heavily on *Tinker* for the rationale (p. 575). Although Faaborg focused on the Third Circuit's decisions in *Seyfried v. Walton*,[11] she provided great insight about concerns over student

---

[11] The article summarized the facts of the case. The musical department at Caesar Rodney High School in Dover, Delaware, selected *Pippin* for the spring musical. The director communicated to the cast that the script would be modified (it was modified because several scenes were considered too sexual in nature for a high school production). A parent read an unmodified version of the script and complained to the president of the board of education. The complaint was passed along to the superintendent. After reviewing a revised version of the script, the superintendent still determined that the production was

expression rights at the time, and drew several conclusions about the federal courts' approach to student speech and expression in school. Unlike Freeman, Faaborg found that *Tinker* stood "for the proposition that student's First Amendment rights can be restricted only when school authorities can demonstrate that the student's conduct materially disrupts or involved substantial disorder in the school environment or invaded the rights of others" (p. 579). Coupled with a recognition of these rights, Faaborg pointed out that school boards and educational leaders have managerial discretion in running schools, and that "the state is free to create an academic environment where teaching and learning will proceed free form disruption" (p. 579). However, she stated that such conduct by school leaders could not violate the constitutional limits set by the Supreme Court.

While Freeman focused on the restrictive nature of the *Tinker* opinion and the power it provided school leaders, Faaborg clearly suggested that Tinker severely hampered the school administrator's ability to limit student speech and expression. She also claimed that student self-expression was at the heart of *Tinker* and that *Tinker* applied First Amendment speech and expression principles to student expressive activities in school, limiting school leaders' ability to quash students' self-expression (p. 580).

As for the actual play at issue, Faaborg focused her analysis on the Third Circuit's characterization of the play as curriculum-related as rationale for upholding the superintendent's censoring of the production. She argued that the federal court's decision implied that there were no limits on the amount of control that school leaders could exert over curricular issues. Faaborg concluded that this approach ignored First

---

inappropriate and directed that it not be performed. Although objection was made to the board of education, the board refused to become involved in the matter.

The district court concluded that the superintendent's decision to cancel the play because it was inappropriate for school sponsorship did not offend the students' expression rights. The Third Circuit Court of Appeals affirmed the decision. The students decided not to appeal to the Supreme Court because they were pessimistic that the Court would overrule the lower courts' decisions (pp. 577-578).

Amendment rights of students and faculty as defined by *Tinker*, and was an incorrect and incomplete analysis of student speech and expression rights. Furthermore, the decision left several issues unresolved, including: (a) what is the test for identifying a student activity as curriculum-related, (b) is a dramatic production protected speech, and (c) is the school auditorium a public forum? Faaborg answered her own questions, and concluded that a school play is *not* a curriculum-related activity, that the production of a play is clearly protected speech, and that the school theater was a limited public forum providing school leaders with some – but limited – ability to regulate the content of school plays (pp. 590-592). Written in 1985 and based on the court decisions at the time, Faaborg's analysis, while extremely critical of the Third Circuit and the limits placed on student expression, was possibly correct.

However, in the next three years, the Supreme Court published two decisions, *Bethel Sch. Dist.* v. *Fraser* (1986) and *Hazelwood Sch. Dist.* v. *Kuhlmeier* (1988), which contradicted points Faaborg put forth in her analysis. *Fraser* established that students' rights are not the same as those of adults outside the school building (*Fraser*, p. 682), and although it did not address school plays specifically, *Kuhlmeier* established a broad definition of curriculum-related activity, which has been interpreted to include school plays (*See gen. Kuhlmeier*, p. 272-273). This gave school leaders great latitude in limiting student expression in the context of school-sponsored or curriculum-related activities. Faaborg's article made compelling arguments with regard to school plays as protected student expression, but twenty-five years later the arguments are still not being utilized or supported by the Court. The article provided a sense of the uncertainty surrounding the exact extent of students' speech and expression rights at the time, and it exemplified many scholars' feelings that students' expression rights should be expanded (and were under *Tinker*), while the lower federal courts, however, were following a trend of limiting students' rights.

The First Amendment to the U.S. Constitution states, in part, "Congress shall make no law ... abridging the freedom of speech, or of the press; or the right of the people peaceably to assemble ... (USCS Const. Amend. 1). In *Tinker*, the Supreme Court articulated that students do not shed their constitutional rights when they enter the schoolhouse (*Tinker*, p. 506). Although this remains true, since *Tinker* the Supreme Court has limited the extent of students' speech and expression rights in school. The Court has concluded that students' rights are not the same as those of adults in other facets of society, and that the special characteristics of the school environment dictate that school leaders may exert more control over student speech and expression on school grounds than student speech offered off school grounds. Points that were made extremely clear in *Fraser* and *Kuhlmeier*.

CHAPTER 2.

Matthew Fraser: Lewd or Just Funny?

As Justice Stevens stated, "[f]rankly, my dear, I don't give a damn" (*Bethel Sch. Dist.* v. *Fraser,* 1986, p. 691), but a majority of the Supreme Court did give a damn about the remarks made by Matthew Fraser during a school assembly. The 128 word speech brought student speech back before the Supreme Court. However, not until 17 years had passed since the Court decided *Tinker.*

Months before the Supreme Court published its decisions in *Fraser,* Dever (1985) reviewed the Ninth Circuit Court of Appeal's application of the Supreme Court's *Tinker* v. *Des Moines Indep. Sch. Dist.* (1969) to *Fraser* v. *Bethel School District* (1985). Dever reviewed the Supreme Court's decision in *Tinker,* and then applied his interpretation of *Tinker* to the facts in *Fraser.*[12] He critiqued the Ninth Circuit's mechanical application of *Tinker* and its conclusion that the school had abridged Fraser's rights because the speech did not materially and substantially disrupt school operations (Dever, p. 1164).

Dever discussed what the Supreme Court would encounter when examined the 128 words utter by Fraser in his campaign speech and decided *Fraser.* Dever argued that although many considered *Tinker* to

---

[12] Matthew Fraser gave a speech during a school assembly in favor of a candidate for a student leadership position. Fraser's speech was characterized as crude and sexually aggressive. The day after giving the speech, Fraser was suspended for violating the school's disruptive conduct policy. Fraser challenged the suspicion using *Tinker* and argued that the speech did not materially and substantially disrupt school (pp. 1168-1169).

be the sole authority for governing student speech in school, the reality was that *Tinker* represented only one of the Court's three approaches to regulating speech: the Public Forum Doctrine (p. 1174).[13] Dever reasoned that by limiting a student expression analysis to *Tinker*, numerous lower federal courts had failed to complete the full Supreme Court First Amendment analysis. Dever was careful to point out that *Tinker* did not expressly rely on the public forum doctrine, but argued that the elements of the doctrine were in the *Tinker* decision (p. 1176). Dever concluded that in *Tinker* the Court first established that the school setting was a limited public forum, and that the material and substantial disruption standard was an alternative way of stating that inappropriate expression is incompatible with the public forum status of the school. Thus, school officials could regulate the expression.

Dever argued that looking at *Tinker* as a public forum doctrine analysis "compels the conclusion that the material and substantial disruption standard is not dispositive on all questions of student speech; rather, it constitutes only one level of inquiry..." (pp. 1176-1177). Such a conclusion, Dever found, meant that courts must look at student expression under *Tinker* but also under terms of Categorical Proscription and Time, Place, and Manner. Dever concluded that this was something that the Ninth Circuit in *Fraser* failed to do, and that the Supreme Court must look at how Fraser's speech was incompatible with the school environment even if it was not disruptive (p. 1177, 1189).

Dever's conclusion regarding *Tinker* was an accurate prediction of the Court's approach in *Fraser*. In deciding that Matthew Fraser's speech was inappropriate and could be punished by school leaders, the Supreme Court moved away from *Tinker* and employed alternative

---

[13] Dever articulated that the Court had actually developed three frameworks for evaluating speech and expression in general. He described the three approaches as: 1. Categorical Proscription, which allows for the regulation of certain types of speech; 2. Time, Place, and Manner Restrictions, which allows for restricting the "physical manner, location, or time of speech communication, not what is being said;" and 3. Public Forum Doctrine, under which the amount of allowable restriction is directly related to the type of forum: public, limited public, and non-public (pp. 1172-1174).

rationale for finding that Fraser's expression fell outside Constitutional protection. The Supreme Court made this clear in *Fraser*, and it was later reinforced in *Morse*, when Chief Justice Roberts stated that *Fraser* provided that *Tinker* was not the only manner for evaluating student expression in school (*Morse v. Frederick, 2007* p. 2627). While Dever was correct in suggesting that federal courts should have been looking beyond the *Tinker* approach when examining student expression in school, he missed the mark when hypothesizing on the rationale the Supreme Court would actually use to decide *Fraser*.

While *Tinker* required the Court to examine constitutional safeguards related to students' right to freedom of expression in school in the form of private and non-disruptive political expression, *Fraser* forced the Court to look at student speech in a different context - the constitutionality of student speech during a school-sponsored activity. In *Bethel Sch. Dist. v. Fraser* (1986), the Court was faced with the question of "whether the First Amendment prohibits a school district from disciplining a high school student for giving a lewd speech at a school assembly" (*Fraser*, p. 677).

During a student council officer election assembly, Fraser delivered a speech in support of a candidate, which was characterized as lewd and obscene and described the candidate in "elaborate, graphic, and explicit sexual metaphors" (*Fraser*, p. 678). The colorful remarks Fraser exclaimed included:

> I know a man who is firm -- he's firm in his pants, he's firm in his shirt, his character is firm -- but most . . . of all, his belief in you, the students of Bethel, is firm. Jeff Kuhlman is a man who takes his point and pounds it in. If necessary, he'll take an issue and nail it to the wall. He doesn't attack things in spurts -- he drives hard, pushing and pushing until finally -- he succeeds. Jeff is a man who will go to the very end -- even the climax, for each and every one of you. So vote for Jeff for A.

S. B. vice-president -- he'll never come between you and the best our high school can be. (*Fraser*, p. 687)[14]

The assembly was considered a "school-sponsored educational program in self-government" and was attended by approximately 600 students, some as young as 14 years old. Prior to giving the speech, Fraser discussed his speech with two teachers and was told he probably should not give the speech. The morning after the assembly, Fraser was notified he had violated the school's disruptive conduct rule prohibiting the use of obscene language. He was given an opportunity to explain his conduct and he admitted to purposely giving the speech and deliberately using sexual innuendo. He was then notified that he would be suspended for three days and his name removed from the list of potential graduation speakers.[15] Fraser served two days of the suspension before returning to school (pp. 678-679).

After exhausting his administrative remedies, Fraser filed suit in the U.S. District Court for the Western District of Washington alleging a violation of his First Amendment right to freedom of speech. The district court held that the school's sanctions violated Fraser's freedom of speech, the school disruptive conduct rule was unconstitutionally vague and overbroad, and that the removal of Fraser's name from the list of possible graduation speakers violated the Due Process Clause of the Fourteenth Amendment. The Ninth Circuit Court of Appeals affirmed the district court's decision and held that Fraser's speech was indistinguishable from the *Tinker* armbands. The Ninth Circuit held that Fraser's speech did not offend the Constitution and was protected by the First Amendment under a *Tinker* analysis. The Supreme Court granted certiorari and reversed (*Fraser*, pp. 679-680).

The Supreme Court held the school district acted within its authority by punishing Matthew Fraser for his "offensively lewd and indecent speech" (p. 685). Further, the Court found that the district

---

[14] Justice Brennan provided the text of Fraser's speech in his concurrence and stated that it was hard to believe it was the same speech described by the majority.

[15] Fraser was elected graduation speaker by write-in vote and delivered a speech at the commencement ceremony.

took appropriate action in disassociating from Fraser to show vulgar and lewd speech or conduct was inconsistent with the fundamental values of public education (pp. 685-688). The Court acknowledged that in *Tinker*, the Supreme Court stated, "Students do not shed their constitutional rights to freedom of speech or expression at the schoolhouse gate" (*Fraser, p.* 680), but the Court went on to express:

> The marked difference between the political 'message' of the armbands in *Tinker* and the sexual content of respondent's speech in this case seems to have been given little weight by the Court of Appeals. In upholding the students' right to engage in a nondisruptive, passive expression of a political viewpoint in *Tinker* this Court was careful to note that the case did 'not concern speech of action that intrudes upon the work of the school or the rights of other students'. It is against this backdrop that ...we consider the level of First Amendment protection accorded to Fraser's utterance and actions before an official high school assembly. (p. 680)

In explaining its rationale, the Court first discussed the purpose of America's public schools, and determined that schools must inculcate students with values and manners of civility, much as Freeman had suggested in 1984. These values included the tolerance of diverse political and religious views, but these "fundamental values" must take into account the sensibilities of other students. This led to the Court's announcement of a balance that must be struck in the school setting: "The undoubted freedom to advocate unpopular and controversial views in schools and classrooms must be balanced against the society's countervailing interest in teaching students the boundaries of socially appropriate behavior" (*Fraser, p.* 681).

In its *Fraser* opinion, the Supreme Court turned to another area of student rights – Fourth Amendment search and privacy – and cited *New Jersey v. T.L.O.* (1985) to reaffirm that students' constitutional rights in public school are not automatically coextensive with adults' constitutional rights. The Court was specifically referring to the idea that although adults may not be prohibited from using offensive or lewd expressions in making what the speaker considers a political statement or expression, students in public school are not necessarily extended the same courtesy (*Fraser*, pp. 682-683). To support this point, the Court pointed to other limits it had established for First Amendment speech, including recognizing an interest in protecting minors form vulgar and offensive language, limiting sexually explicit speech from reaching an unlimited audiences that could contain children, and acknowledging that a school board may remove books from the public school library that are pervasively vulgar (p. 684).

The Court refrained from defining "lewd and vulgar speech." Instead, the Court deferred to local school officials: "The determination of what manner of speech in the classroom or in school assembly is inappropriate properly rests with the school board" (*Fraser*, p. 683). Further, the Court noted, "Schools...may determine that the essential lessons of civil, mature conduct cannot be conveyed in a school that tolerates lewd, indecent, or offensive speech and conduct" (p. 683). The Supreme Court then held that the school district acted well within its authority by sanctioning Fraser for his offensively lewd and indecent speech.

The Court pointed out that unlike in *Tinker*, the sanctions received by Fraser were not related to a political viewpoint: "The First Amendment does not prevent the school officials from determining that to permit a vulgar and lewd speech such as respondent's would undermine the school's basic education mission" (p. 685). The Court made mention of the political context of the speech, but quickly moved away from this component of the case's facts, focusing instead on the school's responsibility to inculcate values and to prevent the disruption of the educational process.

Dissenting to the Court's decisions, Justice Stevens began, "Frankly, my dear, I don't give a damn" (*Fraser*, p. 691). The Clark Gable quote was not an attempt to show that the Justice had no interest in the case, but was used to make the point that standards change over time. Although Clark Gable's statement shocked many people when it was first uttered, Justice Stevens argued that during the mid-1980s Clark Gable, nor Matthew Fraser's, statement might not have been as offensive, and that "a group of judges who are at least two generations and 3,000 miles away from the scene" might not be in the best position to determine what speech is currently lewd or obscene (p. 692).

Beyond stating that there was a possible disconnect between the Court and the general public, especially teenagers, Justice Stevens dissented because of what he considered to be the unfair punishment of a student who was not aware of the possibility of punishment for his actions. The majority concluded that Fraser's due process rights had not been violated because his discussion with two teachers and the student handbook had provided him sufficient warning about the possible consequences and sanction (*Fraser,* p. 686).

Although Justice Stevens agreed that a school should be able to regulate content and style of student speech that is carried out in furtherance of the school's education mission, he stated that if a student was going to be punished for utilizing inappropriate speech, that student is entitled to fair notice of the possible consequences and the prohibited expression. He believed the protections of the First Amendment and the Due Process Clause of the Fourteenth Amendment mandated this conclusion (p. 692).

Despite the dissent, the Court concluded that the school's actions were reasonable and did not violate Fraser's constitutional rights. In the process, the Court distinguished the passive, private, political speech in *Tinker* from lewd speech offered at a school-sanctioned event. The Court held that a school could not only disassociate itself from such speech, but that "the First Amendment did not prevent the school officials from determining that to permit a vulgar and lewd speech...would undermine the school's basic educational mission" (*Fraser,* p. 686). Thus, the Court established the second principle for constitutionally limiting student speech and expression: **School officials may prohibit or suppress student expression that is lewd, uncivil, vulgar, or obscene in the classroom or at school assemblies.**

The Supreme Court decision in *Fraser* changed the way school administrators could limit or suppress student speech and expression. In 1987, Slaff looked specifically at the Court's decision in *Fraser,* and argued that the Court departed from *Tinker* to create a new standard for student speech in school. While it was clear that the Court had done this, Slaff concluded that the Court's decision narrowed students' First Amendment rights in schools, and that the Court considered society's interest in teaching students the realm of appropriate social behavior and relied on this consideration to justify sanctioning Fraser's behavior (p. 208).

Slaff viewed the decision as a departure from the groundwork the Court had laid in *Tinker,* and found that in *Tinker* the Court emphasized that children needed to be able to exercise their Constitutional freedoms. The author stated that under *Tinker*, students could express their views while on school grounds, so long as it was done without materially disrupting and substantially interfering with the operation of the school or education process (p. 211). Slaff argued that the purpose of granting students constitutional rights, in *Tinker* and other cases was to safeguard the liberties of these future adults rather than to provide the children with autonomy (p. 214).

Based on the *Fraser* facts, Slaff believed that had the Court systematically applied *Tinker* because she argued that Fraser's speech would have failed to meet the threshold "material disruption standard" previously established by the Court. Slaff believed the Supreme Court decided to develop a new standard and focus on Fraser's actual speech rather than employ *Tinker*'s substantial disruption standard because of the possible outcome of such an analysis. The Court backed away from *Tinker* and the author concluded that *Fraser* muddied the spectrum of what actually constituted protected student speech and expression versus speech and expression that could be prohibited (p. 221).

Regardless if Slaff's assumptions regarding what was behind the Court's reasoning are correct, the *Fraser* Court, in many ways, did limit the applicability of the *Tinker* analysis to passive student expression. Many educators and scholars, like Slaff, argue that this distinction allowed the Court to determine that the school could regulate offensive speech, such as in *Fraser*, based on the idea that the speech undermined the school's educational mission (p. 215). In doing so, this provided school official another avenue for limiting student speech in the school environment.

Beyond the practical impact of the decision, the Supreme Court's hearing of *Fraser* emphasized the Court's renewed involvement in the realm of public school student's constitutional rights (Thibodeaux, 1987, p. 525). While the Supreme Court had decided a student privacy / search and seizure case the previous year, it had been nearly *two decades* since the Court had examined the issue of student speech rights in school.[16] *Tinker* was the first time the Court evaluated school leaders' actions against the fact that students possessed some First

---

[16] The Supreme Court decided *New Jersey v. T.L.O.* in 1985.

Amendment rights (p. 518) and in *Fraser* the Court was once again faced with a similar issue.

While the situations involved similar issues – student speech in school, the facts of *Tinker* and *Fraser* are easily distinguishable. In *Tinker*, the conduct of the students in wearing the armbands did not intrude upon the rights of other students; however, Fraser's speech placed school officials in the precarious position of having to balance Fraser's "right" to publicly make sexually laced comments against their duty to teach students appropriate social behavior (*see gen. Tinker; Fraser; see also* Thibodeaux, p. 522). The Fraser Court also focused its attention on the young and impressionable age of some students that were in the audience to hear Fraser's speech and the need to protect these students. The Court stated, "[t]he speech could well be seriously damaging to its less mature audience, many of whom were only 14 years old and on the threshold of awareness of human sexuality. Some students were reported as bewildered by the speech and the reaction of mimicry it provoked" (*Fraser*, pp. 683 – 684). Arguably, this rationale also constituted a split from *Tinker* and that First Amendment protections could be dependent on age (*see* Fraser, p. 686). In addition, *Fraser* reestablished the deferential treatment courts should and will show to school leader's decisions.

At the same time, the Court's differentiated approach, added uncertainty and perplexity to what students could actually say or express in school (Thibodeaux, p. 526). "The Court provides no constitutional standard that will guide schools in determining what speech or behavior is appropriate" (Zollo, p. 203).The Court's decision left suppressing student speech and expression that could be considered vulgar to school leader's discretion, but did not dictate what lewd or vulgar actually meant in the school context nor provide a constitutional standard for controlling the discretion (*see Fraser*, p.683; *see also* Zollo, p. 203 - 204). Rather, the Court stated that what constituted inappropriate speech in the classroom or during a school assembly was a decision left to the local board of education (*Fraser*, p. 683).

CHAPTER 3

Extra Extra!!! The Administration Decides if You Read all about It!

Only two years after *Fraser*, the issue of student expression in the context of a school-sponsored activity once again was back before the Supreme Court. Rather than focused on what a student could say, this time the issue focused on what students could write, and the limits of student press and publication in a school-sponsored or endorsed newspaper. In *Hazelwood Sch. Dist.* v. *Kuhlmeier* (1988), the Supreme Court addressed the specific question of the "extent to which educators may exercise editorial control over the contents of a high school newspaper produced as part of the school's journalism curriculum" (p. 262).

Prior to publication of the May 13, 1983 edition of the Hazelwood East High School student paper, *Spectrum*, the administration deleted two pages of articles contained in the paper. In response, three students filed suit against the district alleging that school officials violated their First Amendment rights by deleting the pages. The U.S. District Court for the Eastern District of Missouri held that no First Amendment violation had occurred based in part on the Supreme Court's holding in *Bethel Sch. Dist. v. Fraser*, 478 U.S. 675 (1986). However, the Eighth Circuit Court of Appeals reversed the lower court and held that *Spectrum* was a public forum, which precluded school officials from censoring its content. The Eighth Circuit based its holding on the Court's opinion in *Tinker Des Moines Indep. Cmty. Sch. Dist.* (1969) (*Kuhlmeier*, pp. 263-266). The Supreme Court granted certiorari and reversed the Eighth Circuit.

Spectrum was the typical high school newspaper. It was written and edited by the school's Journalism II class and the board of education had allocated the funds to help pay for the production of the paper. The general practice at Hazelwood East was that prior to publication of the paper, page proofs were submitted to the principal for his review. When Principal Reynolds reviewed the proofs for the May 13th issue, he objected to two of the articles that were slated to appear in the paper. The first story described Hazelwood East students' pregnancy experiences and the second was a story about the impact of divorce on students at the school. Reynolds did not believe the pregnancy story could keep the identity of the pregnant students private, even though the names had been changed. He was also concerned that the information concerning sexual activity and birth control, contained in the article, was inappropriate for younger students.

As for the story concerning divorce, Reynolds believed that a student's derogatory comments about her father, which were included in the article, required that the girl's family should have been contacted and given an opportunity to respond. The article's student author had not contacted the family for comment (*Kuhlmeier*, pp. 262-263). Reynolds felt that there was insufficient time to rewrite the stories and still get the paper to press on time. He directed the Journalism II teacher to withhold the pages containing the articles from the paper, and publish the May 13th edition without the two pages.

As the district court and court of appeals utilized different legal standards to arrive at decisions, the Supreme Court began its opinion by revisiting its decisions concerning student rights and looked not only to student speech and expression precedent, but also to the precedent the Court had established in the context of students' Fourth Amendment rights in *New Jersey v. T.L.O.*, 469 U.S. 325 (1985).[17] Specifically, the

---

[17] T.L.O. was caught in the girls' bathroom at her school. Smoking in the bathroom was a violation of school rules and T.L.O. was taken to the main office where she met with Assistant Principal Choplick. T.L.O., a 14-year-old freshman girl, denied that she had been smoking in the bathroom and stated that she did not smoke. After the denial, Mr. Choplick demanded to see her purse. T.L.O complied and when Choplick looked inside her purse he found a package of cigarettes and noticed a package of rolling papers (*T.L.O.*, p. 328). According to Choplick, in his experience rolling papers suggested use of

Court focused on its announcement in *T.L.O.* that students' right are not coexistent with those of adults, that students' rights must be examined and applied "in light of the special circumstances" inherent in the school context, and drew on its conclusion in *Fraser* that a school is not required to tolerate speech that is inconsistent with the school's education mission (*Kuhlmeier*, p. 266). The Court went on to reiterate that it was the local school board's duty, not the federal court's responsibility, to determine what constitutes inappropriate classroom and school assembly speech. It was against this student speech and expression backdrop that the Hazelwood student's claims had to be considered (p. 267).

The Court first reviewed whether *Spectrum* was a public forum as the Eighth Circuit had concluded. The Court found the evidence relied on by the Eighth Circuit "equivocal at best," and that the school district had neither created nor endorsed *Spectrum* as a public forum (*Kuhlmeier*, p. 269). Before reaching this conclusion, the Court pointed out:

---

marijuana, which he believed meant that a closer examination of the purse would reveal evidence of drug use. Choplick proceeded with a more in-depth search that revealed a small amount of marijuana, a pipe, empty plastic bags, a substantial amount of money in one-dollar bills, a list of student names on an index card, and two letters that implicated T.L.O. in dealing marijuana.

After the search, Choplick notified T.L.O.'s mother and the local police authorities, and turned the confiscated purse contents over to the police. T.L.O.'s mother took her to the police station; once there, T.L.O. confessed to selling marijuana at school. The State of New Jersey, based on the confession and evidence discovered by Choplick, brought delinquency charges against T.L.O. in the Juvenile Court of Middlesex County (p. 328 – 329). After the case was decided at lower court levels, the U.S. Supreme Court granted certiorari to consider the question of whether the Fourth Amendment placed any limits on administrators in conducting searches of students at school. The Court concluded that the Fourth Amendment did limit administrators' authority to conduct searches; however, under the circumstances the search of T.L.O's purse did not violate the Fourth Amendment (p. 332 - 333).

School facilities may be deemed to be public forums only if school authorities have 'by policy or by practice' opened those facilities 'for indiscriminate use by the general public,' or by some segment of the public such as student organizations. If the facilities have instead been reserved for other intended purposes, 'communicative of otherwise,' then no public forum has been created, and school officials may impose reasonable restrictions on the speech of students, teachers and other members of the school community. (p. 267)

The Court's interpretation dictated that a school must take affirmative steps to create a public or limited public forum, and that in this circumstance Hazelwood East had taken no such action.

The Court looked specifically at Hazelwood East's policies and practices related to publication of the student newspaper. The Court determined that *Spectrum* was a component of the curriculum, was defined as such by board policy and the Hazelwood East curriculum guide, and was not a public forum (*Kuhlmeier*, p. 268). The Court pointed out that *Spectrum* was a portion of the curriculum because Journalism II was taught by a school faculty member and students received a grade for their work on *Spectrum*. The Court also found that the district had not deviated from treating *Spectrum* as part of the curriculum because the journalism teacher retained final authority over nearly every aspect of the student newspaper, including content. Further, even after the Journalism teacher approved the paper, Principal Reynolds reviewed the paper before publication. The Court concluded, "School officials did not evince either by policy or by practice" any intent to open the pages of *Spectrum* to "indiscriminate use by its student reporters and editors, or by the student body generally" (p. 270). The school utilized the paper as a supervised learning experience for students in Journalism II. The Court stated that it was this standard, rather than the holding in *Tinker*, that gave school officials the ability and right to regulate the content of *Spectrum* in a reasonable manner.

The majority and the dissent agreed that the Court's decision parted ways with the standard established in *Tinker*. The majority explained the distinction and need for a different approach because of the different questions addressed in the cases:

The question whether the First Amendment requires a school to tolerate particular speech...is different from the question whether the First Amendment requires a school affirmatively to promote particular student speech...The latter question concerns educators authority over school-sponsored publications...that students, parents, and member of the public might reasonably perceive to bear the imprimatur of the school. These activities may fairly be characterized as part of the school curriculum. (pp. 270 -271)

The Court articulated three reasons for educators exercising greater control over the second type of student speech and expression: (a) to insure that students learn the lessons the class or activity intended to teach, (b) to safeguard against learners being exposed to information and material that is inappropriate for their maturity, and (c) to prohibit an individual speaker's view from being attributed to the school (p. 271). The Court went on to explain that schools need authority to set high standards for student speech that is published or communicated "under its auspices" (p. 271). The standards may be higher than those utilized in the public, and schools have the right to refuse to disseminate student speech that does not reach these standards (pp. 271-272).

Without giving schools this freedom and without giving students a raised level of responsibility, the Court opined that schools would be unduly constrained in fulfilling their role of helping students adjust to their environment, assisting in their educational development, and stimulating their cultural awareness (*Kuhlmeier*, p. 272.). The Court concluded that the *Tinker* standard did not need to be the standard utilized when determining "when a school may refuse to lend its name and resources to the dissemination of student expression" (p. 272). In place of the *Tinker* standard, the Court held that "educators do not offend the First Amendment by exercising editorial control over the style and content of student speech in school-sponsored expressive activities so long as their actions are reasonably related to legitimate pedagogical concerns" (p. 273).

The Court reasoned that this new standard respected the view that the primary responsibility of educating students rests with the local school board, teachers, and parents. "It is only when the decision to censor a school-sponsored publication...has no valid educational purpose that the *First Amendment* is so directly and sharply implicated as to require judicial intervention to protect students' constitutional rights" (*Kuhlmeier*, p. 273). This new position dictated judicial action that was almost in direct contradiction of the Court's opinion in *Tinker*, where the Court announced that a school could censor student expression *only* if "it materially disrupts class work or involves substantial disorder or invasion of the rights of others" (*Tinker*, p. 513). Less than 20 years after *Tinker*, the Court had gone from protecting private student expression rights and limiting when a school *could* interfere to announcing that the courts will only step in to curb school censorship when the censorship of student expression in a school-sponsored publication is not "reasonably related to a legitimate pedagogical concern" (*Kuhlmeier*, p. 273).

Justice Brennan, in his dissenting opinion, acknowledged the break from *Tinker*, but argued it was not needed. He argued that the Court applied the *Tinker* test to *Fraser*, but instead of continuing to utilize *Tinker*, the *Kuhlmeier* majority created a dichotomy in which *Tinker* applied to one type of expression but not to another. Brennan believed that *Tinker* should have been utilized because under *Tinker,* the school still had the freedom to "constitutionally censor poor grammar, writing, or research because to reward such expression would 'materially disrupt' the newspaper's curricular purpose (Brennan dissent, p. 284). Justice Brennan's position, however, assumed that a break had not already occurred from *Tinker*: "From the first sentence of its analysis, *Fraser* faithfully applied *Tinker*" (p. 282), the majority of the *Kuhlmeier* Court did not share this opinion.

In fact, The *Kuhlmeier* majority did not even thoroughly address the applicability of the *Tinker* analysis to the facts of *Fraser*, merely noting Justice Brennan's argument in a footnote.[18] However, the

---

[18] The majority in *Morse* v. *Frederick* (2007), 20 years after *Kuhlmeier* and the next Supreme Court student speech decision, also took issue with Justice Brennan's stance stating that the Court broke from *Tinker* in *Fraser* and then the *Kuhlmeier* majority established a *third* student speech standard (*Morse*, p. 2626). Justice Thomas' concurrence in *Morse* also noted the move away from

majority did point out that the *Fraser* decision rested on the lewd and vulgar character of a speech delivered at a school-sponsored event, cited the *dissent* from *Tinker* as support for the Court's decision in *Fraser* (*Kuhlmeier*, p. 271, ftnt. 4), and indicated that the *Fraser* majority had moved away from a strict *Tinker* analysis. Thus, the Supreme Court's holding in *Kuhlmeier* created a third distinct standard for addressing students' First Amendment speech and expression rights in school, not merely a dichotomy as Justice Brennan's dissent suggested.

Utilizing this third approach for addressing student speech and expression in school, the Court concluded that under the particular circumstances of the case Principal Reynolds acted reasonably and had not violated the students' speech and expression rights. The Court believed that the identifying information in the pregnancy article potentially violated any pledge of anonymity given to the subject of the article, that it was reasonable for the principal to be concerned about the content of the article being inappropriate for the younger students, and that it was reasonable for the principal to believe that the father discussed in the divorce article was entitled to an opportunity to defend himself (*Kuhlmeier*, pp. 274-275). Further, the time constraints relating to publication made the principal's decision to exclude the pages containing the articles reasonable. "In sum, we cannot reject as unreasonable Principal Reynolds' conclusion that neither... article...was suitable for publication in *Spectrum*...the principal's decision to delete two pages of *Spectrum*...was reasonable ... Accordingly no violation of First Amendment rights occurred" (p. 276).

In the three years prior to the Supreme Court's *Kuhlmeier* decision, the Eighth Circuit decided two cases concerning prior restraint and a school's ability to censor student speech or expression when it is expressed in the context of a school-sponsored publication or event. In the case of *Kuhlmeier*, the Eighth Circuit held that a school could not censor student speech because the school had created an open forum, stating that the school violated student free speech and expression rights when it deleted two pages of the school-sponsored student

---

Tinker in *Fraser*: "Distancing itself from *Tinker's* approach, the *Fraser* Court quoted Justice Black's dissent in *Tinker*" (*Morse*, p. 2634).

newspaper (*Kuhlmeier* v. *Hazelwood Sch. Dist.*, p. 1374, 8th Cir. 1987). In *Bystrom et al.* v. *Fridley High School et al.* (1987), the Eighth Circuit upheld a school policy that gave school administrators the right to review publications prior to distribution on the school's campus. The decision spoke only to the facial constitutionality of the particular school policy governing review before distribution (p. 755).[19]

Six months after *Bystrom*, the Supreme Court published *Kuhlmeier* and provided a new standard: when the school has not affirmatively designated a school publication, activity, or program a public forum, "educators do not offend the First Amendment by exercising editorial control over the style and content of student speech in school-sponsored expressive activities so long as their actions are reasonably related to legitimate pedagogical concerns" (*Kuhlmeier*, p. 273). This is a prime example of the Supreme Court taking an issue that has been decided in a variety of ways by lower courts and providing a set standard that all courts (and schools) must - or are supposed to – adhere to.

Almost immediately after the Court published its *Kuhlmeier* opinion, academics and educators began discussing what many considered a further limiting of student speech rights; however, a fierce split developed over whether this was good or bad for education. Abrams and Goodman (1988) published one of the early responses to the Court's decisions. Abrams and Goodman addressed how the Court had changed the censorship standard for expression. Prior to *Kuhlmeier*, they argued, the standard for censorship had been substantial disruption; however, following *Kuhlmeier* the broad guidelines for limiting student speech and expression had been modified to allow editorial control of student publications if the control is reasonably related to a legitimate pedagogical interest (p. 274). This position specifically tracked the rationale given by the Supreme Court (*Kuhlmeier*, p. 273). However, Abrams and Goodman believed *Kuhlmeier* actually represented a case of viewpoint suppression because the Court made an unnecessary change to the substantial disruption standard, established in *Tinker*, resulting in broad control of student speech and expression by school leaders (Abrams and

---

[19] Bystrom is discussed in more detail in Chapter 7.

Extra Extra!!!   39

Goodman, p. 725). The decision was viewed by many as allowing
school leaders to censor student publications and reduce learning
opportunities available to students (*See* Abrams and Goodman, *see also*
Boggs, 2005).

Abrams and Goodman were not alone in their thinking, as Buss
(1989) drew very similar conclusions regarding the Supreme Court's
work in *Kuhlmeier*. In discussing the relation between *Tinker* and
Kuhlmeier, Buss conclude:

> The *Hazelwood* decision is best explained in terms of the
> school's power to control its communicative resources, rather
> than as a power to regulate student speech. *Tinker* and
> *Hazelwood* are different in kind, not degree. In muting this
> distinction, the Court is taking a misleading step that could
> become a foot in the door for regulating student speech
> protected by *Tinker*. (p. 513)

Like numerous other academics, Buss viewed *Kuhlmeier* as
limiting student expression and encouraged further limiting of student
expression. .Scholars saw *Kuhlmeier* as a warning that nearly any
forum for public expression in school could be limited or narrowed
based on the specific circumstances and school administration's
prerogative.

The *Kuhlmeier* decision also revitalized the debate regarding the
inculcative function of the public school system. Like Freeman (1984)
in the wake of *T.L.O.*, Lane (1992) addressed the extent of student
rights in school in relation to the inculcative function of the public
school system (p. 24) with the addition of *Kuhlmeier* to the Court's
resume of student rights' decisions. At the heart of the debate are two
competing ideas: student autonomy and social integration in school (p.
46, 70). Social integration views children as needing guidance and the
school is charged with a responsibility of ensuring students receive
certain protections (p. 71 – 72), while student autonomy emphasis
choice and provide students more freedom (p. 74).

Kuhlmeier in many ways speaks directly to this debate. The
Court's decision supports the view that children need guidance in terms
of what is appropriate as they acclimate into society. Providing students
"protection" by allowing principals and other school authorities to

regulate the content of school publications in many ways can be interpreted as shielding students from the potential repercussions of ill advised, slanderous, or inappropriate articles (*see Kuhlmeier*, p. 273 – 276). However, while providing students with additional autonomy would potentially expose students to liability for poor decisions related to published material, it would also give these students more freedom (Lane, p. 74). The *Kuhlmeier* Court clearly valued protecting students over providing them expanded opportunity.

While this seems extremely parental, the Supreme Court has long held that children's constitutional rights do not mirror those of adults. In 1944, the Supreme Court established a lower threshold of constitutional rights for children (*Prince v. Massachusetts*, 1944). In *Prince*, the Court held that school leaders may regulate students' to a greater extent than government leaders' may regulate adults in society (Lane, p. 77 - 78). While articulating it somewhat differently, the Court reiterated this position in *T.L.O.* and *Fraser* when it stated that students' rights do not mirror those of adults in the rest of society (*Morse*, p.2627 citing *Fraser*).

While some scholars such as Lane have been critical of the protective approach because while children can be immature and need protection, they must also be allowed to grow into adults (p.88), some argued "it is in children's and society's best interests to limit children's short-term legal autonomy in order to facilitate development of their long-term actual autonomy" (Hafen and Hafen, 1995, p. 307). A conclusion that is based on the idea that a premature granting of legal autonomy could undercut a child's development of actual autonomy as adults (p. 385). While the *Tinker* decision originally suggested expansive autonomy for students, *Fraser* and *Kuhlmeier* not only limited student speech but autonomy too. and restored the school's right to limit student freedom in order to allow schools the freedom to do what they were established to do (pp. 386-387).

While *Kuhlmeier* did further limit student speech in schools, it did not completely eliminate student speech rights in school. Numerous decisions handed down after *Kuhlmeier* still protected private student speech that is not disruptive, which is to be expected as the Supreme Court clearly articulated that *Kuhlmeier* represented an additional approach to addressing the appropriateness of certain student speech in school (*see Morse*, p. 2626). *Kuhlmeier* did provide schools the discretion to regulate the content of the school newspaper; however, some lower courts found the decision – on the facts – inapplicable to student newspaper cases. For example, in *Desilets v. Clearview Regional Board of Education* (1994), a New Jersey court distinguished *Kuhlmeier* concluding that the school failed to show a valid educational purpose for censorship when it attempted to exclude a student's review of two movies from the school paper because the movies were rated R. Thus, *Kuhlmeier* does provide school administrators greater latitude in regulating student speech offered in the course of school-sponsored actives or publications, it did not grant school leaders carte blanch censorship authority. Furthermore, while school leaders may limit speech based on legitimate pedagogical reasons, school could not participate in blatant viewpoint discrimination (McCarthy, 1998, p.21). The *Kuhlmeier* Court drew a clear distinction between tolerated personal student expression and school promotion of student speech that could be reasonably interpreted as representing the school, which the school could censor.

Beating Back Kuhlmeier

In response to the limitations *Kuhlmeier* placed on student speech and press rights in school, numerous states have passed statutes, which grant students' freedom of the press rights that extend beyond the limited rights established in *Kuhlmeier*. The laws have been nicknamed "anti-Hazelwood statutes". Arkansas has adopted a chapter governing student press titled the "Arkansas Student Publication Act" (*see* ARK. CODE ANN. §§6-18-1201 to -1204, 2008), which specifically provides "Student publications policies shall recognize that students may exercise their right of expression, within the framework outlined in § 6-18-1202. This right includes expression in school-sponsored publications, whether such publications are supported financially by the school or by use of school facilities, or are produced in conjunction with a class" (A.C.A. § 6-18-1203, 2008).

The California student press statute provides, in part "Students of the public schools shall have the right to exercise freedom of speech and of the press…whether or not such publications or other means of expression are supported financially by the school or by use of school facilities, except that expression shall be prohibited which is obscene, libelous, or slanderous…Student editors of official school publications shall be responsible for assigning and editing the news, editorial, and feature content of their publications subject to the limitations of this section. However, it shall be the responsibility of a journalism adviser or advisers of student publications within each school to supervise the production of the student staff, to maintain professional standards of English and journalism, and to maintain the provisions of this section. There shall be no prior restraint of material prepared for official school publications except insofar as it violates this section. School officials shall have the burden of showing justification without undue delay prior to any limitation of student expression under this section. "Official school publications" refers to material produced by students in the journalism, newspaper, yearbook, or writing classes and distributed to the student body either free or for a fee" (CAL. EDUC. CODE § § 48907, 2008).

The Colorado General Assembly codified public school students' publication rights. The statute specifically states: "students of the public schools shall have the right to exercise freedom of speech and of the press, and no expression contained in a student publication, whether or not such publication is school-sponsored, shall be subject to prior restraint except for the types of expression described in subsection (3) of this section ... Nothing in this section shall be interpreted to authorize the publication or distribution in any media by students of the following: (a) expression that is obscene; (b) expression that is libelous, slanderous, or defamatory under state law; (c) expression that is false as to any person who is not a public figure or involved in a matter of public concern; or (d) expression that creates a clear and present danger of the commission of unlawful acts, the violation of lawful school regulations, or the material and substantial disruption of the orderly operation of the school or that violates the rights of others to privacy or that threatens violence to property or persons." The Colorado General Assembly further directed that if a student publication is made generally available the publication will be designated a public forum (COLO. REV. STAT. § 22-1-120, 2008).

Iowa has granted student journalist broad freedom with limited exceptions. "Students of the public schools have the right to exercise freedom of speech, including the right of expression in official school publications. 2. Students shall not express, publish, or distribute any of the following: *a.* Materials which are obscene. *b.* Materials which are libelous or slanderous under chapter 659. *c.* Materials which encourage students to do any of the following: (1) Commit unlawful acts. (2) Violate lawful school regulations. (3) Cause the material and substantial disruption of the orderly operation of the school." The statute further established that there would be no prior restraint by school officials except if the publication violated the guidelines provided in the statute, and student editors have content control over publications. The statute also disassociated the school from the student expression in the publication; "any expression made by students in the exercise of free speech, including student expression in official school publications, shall not be deemed to be an expression of school policy, and the public school district and school employees or officials shall not be liable in any civil or criminal action for any student expression made or published by students" (IOWA CODE § 280.22, 2007).

The Kansas Student Publication Act provides "liberty of the press in student publications shall be protected. School employees may regulate the number, length, frequency, distribution and format of student publications. Material shall not be suppressed solely because it involves political or controversial subject matter." Like Iowa, the act provided that student expression in school-sponsored student-created publications was not an expression of the school (KAN. STAT. ANN. § 72-1504 to -1506, 2008).

Massachusetts provides, "The right of students to freedom of expression in the public schools of the commonwealth shall not be abridged, provided that such right shall not cause any disruption or disorder within the school. Freedom of expression shall include without limitation, the rights and responsibilities of students, collectively and individually, (a) to express their views through speech and symbols, (b) to write, publish and disseminate their views, (c) to assemble peaceably on school property for the purpose of expressing their opinions. Any assembly planned by students during regularly scheduled school hours shall be held only at a time and place approved in advance by the school principal or his designee. No expression made by students in the exercise of such rights shall be deemed to be an expression of school policy and no school officials shall be held responsible in any civil or criminal action for any expression made or published by the students. For the purposes of this section and sections eighty-three to eighty-five, inclusive, the word student shall mean any person attending a public secondary school in the commonwealth. The word school official shall mean any member or employee of the local school committee" (MASS. GEN. LAWS ANN. ch. 71, § 82, 2008).

Each of these states has adopted laws that expand student speech, expression, and press rights. Although states have the constitutional right to pass laws and regulations that grant students more freedom than those provided by the Supreme Court and the federal Constitution, states *cannot* pass measures that articulate student rights in a manner that is more restrictive than the protections the Constitution provides, as determined by the Supreme Court. While this approach is well within a state's rights, it does not affect the realm of students' speech rights under the 1st Amendment to the U.S. Constitution.

Three of a Kind

Kuhlmeier created a third principle for evaluating students' speech and expression rights and responsibilities. Instead of articulating it in terms of students' rights, the Court announced the new approach in terms of school officials' rights: **School leaders may exercise "editorial control over the style and content of student speech in school-sponsored expressive activities so long as their actions are reasonably related to legitimate pedagogical concerns"** (*Kuhlmeier*, pp. 272-273). This further limited students' speech and expression rights in school and specifically established that students were not free to publish articles in curriculum related newspapers concerning any issue they wished. In broad terms, it gave school leaders great latitude in controlling student expression that was voiced or published during a school-sponsored or curriculum-related activity.

CHAPTER 4.

Back to Black

Twenty years after he filed his dissenting opinion in *Tinker*, Justice Black's *Tinker* dissent was cited in the next two student speech and expression cases addressed by the Supreme Court. The Court had limited student expression in *Fraser* and *Kuhlmeier* in a manner that was somewhat consistent with his dissent in *Tinker*. Justice Black stated:

> The crucial remaining questions are whether students and teachers may use the schools at their whim as a platform for the exercise of free speech – 'symbolic' or 'pure' – and whether the courts will allocate to themselves the function of deciding how the pupils' school day will be spent...I have never believed that any person has a right to give speeches or engage in demonstrations where he pleases and when he pleases. (Black dissent, p. 517)

Although the second question seemed included for dramatic effect, the *Fraser* and *Kuhlmeier* majority opinions reiterated that the primary responsibility for educating students, making decisions concerning the content of curriculum, and determining what manner of speech is inappropriate in the classroom or at a school-sponsored event rests with the local school officials rather than the courts (*Fraser* p. 683; *Kuhlmeier*, p. 273). The *Fraser* and *Kuhlmeier* decisions also answered Justice Black's first question; the answer was no.

Students and teachers are not unconditionally allowed to utilize the school as a platform for exercising their First Amendment free speech and expression rights. Justice Black warned that the *Tinker* decision would subject all public schools "to the whims and caprices of their loudest-mouthed, but maybe not their brightest, students" (*Tinker*, p. 525). Years later, the Supreme Court was faced with this exact situation and addressed Justice Black's fear in the form of Matthew Fraser. Although Fraser might not fit the description of the student Black provided, the point that Justice Black was attempting to communicate materialized in Fraser's sexually laced campaign speech. Fraser was a well-liked student that offered a speech of questionable taste after being warned that it was inappropriate. When he was punished for it, Fraser wrapped himself in the rationale of *Tinker* for protection.

To free itself of *Tinker's* reach and to condemn Fraser's behavior, the *Fraser* Court turned to Justice Black for the proposition that "the Federal Constitution [does not] compel teachers, parents, and elected school officials to surrender control of the American public school system to public school students" (*Fraser*, p. 686 quoting *Tinker* dissent, p. 526). In holding that the school could sanction Fraser for offensively lewd and indecent speech and could separate itself from student expression that is vulgar and lewd, *Fraser* embraced principles articulated by Justice Black in his *Tinker* dissent. Black offered, and the *Fraser* Court reiterated through its holding, "the truth is that…[a] high school pupil no more carries into a school with him a complete right to freedom of speech and expression than" any person to enter into the Supreme Court or the Senate "contrary to their rules and speak his mind on any subject he pleases" (*Tinker* dissent, pp. 521-522).

The *Kuhlmeier* Court also restricted student speech and expression rights in a manner that was consistent with arguments first articulated by Justice Black. Justice Black reasoned, "Children had not yet reached the point of experience and wisdom which enabled them to teach all of their elders…taxpayers send their children to school on the premise that at their age they need to learn, not teach" (p. 522). Although speaking in the context of political expression and about Iowa schools, Justice Black stated,

> Public schools…are operated to give students an opportunity
> to learn, not talk politics by actual speech, or by 'symbolic'
> speech…here the Court should accord Iowa educational
> institutions the…right to determine for themselves to what
> extent free expression should be allowed in schools. (p. 524)

Although not citing this point, (possibly because the Court was announcing a different test from *Tinker*), the *Kuhlmeier* Court made a strong statement regarding who maintained authority inside the school, ""It is *only when* the decision to censor a school-sponsored publication...has *no valid educational purpose* that the *First Amendment* is so directly and sharply implicated as to require judicial intervention to protect students' constitutional rights" (*Kuhlmeier*, p. 273, emphasis added). This approach by the *Kuhlmeier* Court falls squarely in line with Justice Black's statements. The *Kuhlmeier* Court articulated legitimate pedagogical reasons for restricting student press when such a program (the school newspaper) was developed as part of a curriculum, (i.e., as a learning tool for students), and school officials could reasonably restrict student speech and expression in that forum (*Kuhlmeier*, p. 267). Further, the Court again stated that the main responsibility for educating students rested with the school board and local school authorities, not with the courts (p.273).

Two decades after Justice Black expressed concerns about giving students too much First Amendment speech and expression freedom, the Supreme Court had restricted the freedoms Justice Black opposed when they were originally granted. *Kuhlmeier* gave schools "broad authority to define and supervise students' education, including the right to regulate the content of school-sponsored student newspapers" (Hafen & Hafen, 1995, p. 394). Furthermore, it distinguished private student expression – protected by *Tinker* – from student expression in a school-sponsored activity or publication (p. 394). Since *Kuhlmeier* and *Fraser*, the amount of student expression governed by *Tinker* has been reduced drastically and the fears expressed by Black somewhat limited. Although *Tinker's* material disruption standard still governs "personal *student expression* of ideological views" (McCarthy, 1998, p. 23), this realm of student speech has grown drastically smaller in the school setting because even if the speech was permitted (and protected) under *Tinker*, a student could still be penalized later if the speech was disruptive, defamatory, vulgar or contrary to a legitimate pedagogical interest (if offered during a curriculum related or school-sponsored activity) based on *Fraser* or *Kuhlmeier*. After the Court published *Kuhlmeier*, the pendulum of student speech had swung back much closer to the position championed by Justice Black, and 19 years would pass before the Supreme Court would once again revisit student speech and expression in school.

CHAPTER 5.

No Bong HiTS for Students ... or Jesus

On January 24, 2002, the Olympic torch passed through Juneau, Alaska, and proceeded along a street in front of Juneau-Douglas High School (JDHS). The school's principal, Deborah Morse, permitted students and school staff to participate in the Torch Relay as a sanctioned school activity. Students were excused from classes to watch the torch relay, while teachers and administrators watched and monitored student actions. Joseph Frederick, a JDHS senior, stood with a group of friends across the street facing the school to watch the torch relay. "As the torchbearers and camera crews passed by, Frederick and his friends unfurled a 14-foot banner bearing the phrase: BONG HiTS 4 JESUS" (*Morse v. Frederick*, 2007, p. 2622).

After seeing the banner, Principal Morse immediately approached the students and told them to take the banner down; all of the students complied except Frederick. She told Frederick to report to her office. After meeting with him, Morse suspended Frederick for 10 days. Frederick appealed the suspension and the school district superintendent upheld the suspension but limited it to 8 days, which he had already served (p. 2623).

Frederick filed suit against the school district and Morse in the U.S. District Court for the District of Alaska, claiming that Morse and the school board violated his First Amendment rights. The district court granted Morse and the board summary judgment finding that they had not infringed Frederick's First Amendment rights. The Ninth Circuit Court of Appeals reversed this finding, holding that the district violated Frederick's First Amendment rights because "the school punished Frederick without demonstrating that his speech gave rise to a risk of substantial disruption" (*Morse*, p. 2623). The Supreme Court granted certiorari on two questions: (a) did Frederick have a First Amendment right to display his banner, and (b) if so, was the right so clearly established that Morse may be held liable for damages. The Supreme Court found that Frederick did not have a constitutional right to display the "BONG HiTS 4 JESUS" banner, which dictated that the Court did not need to decide the second question (p. 2625).

Frederick argued that the case did not involve an in-school student speech and expression issue because the events took place across the street from the school. However, the Court determined that Frederick's speech was school-related. The Court identified six factors that showed Frederick's speech was school-related: (a) he was at an event that occurred during normal school hours, (b) the principal approved the students attending the event, (c) district rules specifically stated that students attending approved social events or field trips are subject to school rules,[20] (d) teachers and administrators supervised the students, (e) the high school band and cheerleaders performed, and (f) the superintendent argued, "Frederick cannot stand in the midst of his fellow students, during school hours, at a school-sanctioned activity and claim he is not at school" (p. 2624). The Court agreed with the superintendent's argument. Not only did the Court find that the banner was school-related speech, it went on to state that the facts of *Morse* did not even present a close case that approached the area of "uncertainty at the outer boundaries" of the Court's school-speech jurisprudence (*Morse*, p. 2624).[21]

While the event was determined to be school sponsored, the meaning of Fredrick's banner was still at issue. Frederick claimed that "BONG HiTS 4 JESUS" was simply nonsensical, created to attract the attention of the television cameras. The dissent argued that the message

---

[20] The school rules referred to by the Court are Juneau School Board Policy No. 5520: "The Board specifically prohibits any assembly or public expression that...advocates the use of substances that are illegal to minors;" and No. 5850: "pupils who participate in approved social events and class trips" to the same student conduct rules that apply during the regular school program" (p. 2623).

[21] The Court did not discuss what constituted the "outer boundaries" of its school-speech jurisprudence.

could be characterized as anything from obscure to silly to stupid. While the majority acknowledged nonsensical gibberish was a "possible interpretation of the words on the banner, but not the only one, suggesting that dismissing the banner as meaningless ignores its undeniable reference to illegal drugs" (*Morse*, p. 2625). The Court concluded that at least two interpretations of the banner endorsed or advocated illegal drug use. Principal Morse advanced these two interpretations and the Court embraced both theories. The message could either be seen as "an imperative: [Take] bong hits," or viewed as "celebrating drug use – bong hits [are a good thing] or [we take] bong hits." The Court viewed both interpretations as promoting the use of illegal drugs (p. 2625).

Although It had established that Frederick's "BONG HiTS 4 JESUS" banner was speech, and constituted speech related to a school event, and promoted drug use, the Court did not take these findings are evaluate them against the backdrop of *Tinker, Fraser,* or *Hazelwood*. Rather, the Supreme Court articulated a new narrower issue: "[t]he question becomes whether a principal may, consistent with the First Amendment, restrict student speech at a school event, when that speech is reasonably viewed as promoting illegal drug use. We hold that she may" (*Morse*, p. 2625).

As the Court had once again added to the student speech analysis, the Court revisited what it had established in the different quadrants of the student speech rubric. The Court stated two points from *Tinker*. First, "the Court made clear that First Amendment rights, applied in light of the special characteristics of the school environment" are retained by students when they enter the school building, and second, student expression may not be suppressed unless "school officials reasonably conclude that it will materially and substantially disrupt the work and discipline of the school" (*Morse*, p. 2626).

The Court then turned to *Fraser* and *Kuhlmeier* and the manner in which these decisions had limited the breadth of *Tinker*. In looking at *Fraser*, the *Morse* Court noted that the mode of interpretation utilized by the Court was not clear because the *Fraser* Court focused on the content of Fraser's speech, but also stated that school boards have the authority to decide the manner of speech that is inappropriate in classrooms or school assemblies. The *Morse* Court reasoned that it did not need to resolve the debate regarding the approach taken by the

Court in *Fraser*; instead, the Court pointed to *Fraser*'s holding that student's constitutional rights in school are not coexistent with adult's rights in other settings and that *Fraser* established that the *Tinker* analysis was not absolute (p. 2627).[22] In looking at *Kuhlmeier*, the Court found that *Kuhlmeier* was not controlling because a reasonable person could not conclude the "BONG HiTS 4 JESUS" banner was a school publication or school-sponsored or endorsed expression. However, the *Kuhlmeier* decision was still influential because it held that school officials could regulate speech in school that could not be regulated outside the school context, and confirmed that *Tinker* was not the only basis for restricting student speech and expression in school (p. 2627).

The Court also referred to its student privacy and random drug testing decisions. The Court referenced these decisions as support for designating the increasing drug problem and schools' battle against illegal drug use by students as a legitimate pedagogical concern. "The cases [*New Jersey* v. *T.L.O.*, 1985; *Vernonia Sch. Dist. 47J* v. *Acton*, 1995; and *Brd. of Edu.* v. *Earls*, 2002][23] also recognize that deterring

---

[22] The Court noted, "Whatever approach *Fraser* employed, it certainly did not conduct the substantial disruption analysis prescribed by *Tinker*" (p. 2627).

[23] The cases Justice Roberts referenced, *T.L.O.*, *Acton*, and *Earls*, constitute the Supreme Court's three major decisions concerning the extent of students' privacy rights and Fourth Amendment protections in school.

Vernonia School District 47J (Vernonia) implemented a suspicionless drug testing program for all students involved in district athletic programs. The program was put in place to combat what the district saw as a sharp increase in student drug use, and Vernonia believed student athletes were at the forefront of the drug problem. The program required athletes to sign a consent form for the testing program and obtain written parental consent. Athletes were tested at the beginning of the athletic season and then 10% of the athletes were selected randomly each week to participate in a drug test. The urinalysis drug test required students to enter an empty locker room accompanied by an adult monitor, and male students (fully clothed) produced a sample while standing at a urinal being observed by the monitor standing 12 – 15 feet way. Female students produced a sample in a bathroom stall while the monitor stood outside the stall (*Acton*, p. 650).

drug use by schoolchildren is an 'important – indeed, perhaps compelling' interest" (*Morse,* p. 2628).[24] Based on these decisions, the

---

Seven years after that the decision concerning the Vernonia School District drug testing policy, which was limited to suspicionless drug testing of student athletes, the Court examined the Pottawatomie County School District's drug policy, which allowed for the testing of any student "who participate in competitive extracurricular activities to submit to drug testing" (*Board of Education of Independent School District No. 92 of Pottawatomie County v. Earls,* 2002, p. 825). Justice Thomas delivered the opinion of the Court in *Earls,* and "because this Policy reasonably serves the School District's important interest in detecting and preventing drug use among its students," the Court held it was constitutional (Earls, p. 825).

The school district policy required "all middle and high school students to consent to drug testing in order to participate in any extracurricular activity" (p. 826). The policy required students to undergo a drug test prior to participation in an extracurricular activity, submit to random drug tests while participating, and agree to a test upon reasonable suspicion. The urinalysis drug test was designed to detect only illegal drugs, not medical conditions or prescription drugs.

[24] In *Fraser, Kuhlmeier,* and *Morse,* the Supreme Court turned to precedent it had established in the context of its students' Fourth Amendment rights decisions to support points being made in the context of student speech and expression in school. Likewise, the Court has relied on points from its speech and expression cases when making determinations in the student search and privacy context. Justice Roberts in his majority opinion in *Morse* specifically stated:

Drawing on the principles applied in our student speech cases, we have held in the Fourth Amendment context that while children assuredly do not shed their constitutional rights...at the schoolhouse gate...the nature of those rights is what is appropriate for children in school. In particular the school setting requires some easing of the restrictions to which searches by public authorities are ordinarily subject. Even more to the point, these cases also recognize that deterring drug use by schoolchildren is an important – indeed, perhaps compelling interest. (pp. 2627-2628, internal citations omitted).

Morse Court found that student speech and expression at a school event endorsing illegal drug use posed a legitimate and serious challenge for school officials trying to protect students from the dangers of illegal drugs. After articulating the influences of its past student rights decisions, the Court created a new category of student expression that could be reasonably and constitutionally restricted. The Court held, "The special circumstances of the school environment and the government interest in stopping student drug use...allow schools to restrict student expression that they reasonably regard as promoting illegal drug use" (p. 2629). The Court established that a particular viewpoint – endorsement of illegal drug use – expressed by students in school or at school related activities could reasonably and constitutionally be censored and sanctioned by school officials without running afoul of the First Amendment.

Although in agreement with the Court's decision, Justice Alito, joined by Justice Kennedy, wrote separately to emphasize that the Court's decision:

> Goes no further than to hold that a public school may restrict speech that a reasonable observer would interpret as advocating illegal drug use and (b) it provides no support for any restriction of speech that can plausibly be interpreted as commenting on any political or social issue. (*Morse*, p. 2636)

Justice Alito specifically included social and political commentary concerning the war on drugs and the legalization of marijuana as areas to which the court's decision did not extend. This concurrence is key because it emphasizes Justice Alito's position, which provided the majority its needed votes, that *Morse* is an extremely narrow holding. The decision only provides school leaders with the ability to suppress student expression, in the school setting, that *promotes* illegal drug use

---

This exemplifies the cross-over between areas of student rights jurisprudence. It also highlights the Court's willingness to utilize principles developed in one area to other student rights circumstances.

(p. 2636). It did not provide educators (or courts) the foundation to suppress any and all student speech or expression based on content or specifically about illegal drugs.

In the interim between the Court hearing oral arguments in *Morse* and the publication of the decision, McCarthy (2007) provided an assessment of the current climate of student expression in schools and accurately described the frustration and difficulty of appropriately and uniformly applying the Court's three previous student expression decisions. In interpreting the "Supreme Court Trilogy" – *Tinker*, *Fraser*, and *Kuhlmeier*, the lower federal courts had recognized three distinct forms of student expression: 1. school-sponsored (*Kuhlmeier*), 2. Obscene, lewd, vulgar, or plainly offensive (*Fraser*), and 3. Expression that falls in neither category (*Tinker*). McCarthy described the aggravation and confusion the lower courts' application of these principles has caused school leaders:

> These categories are deceptively discreet and have been referred to in numerous recent cases. Yet, **courts have not spoken with a single voice as to what expression falls in each category or how to apply the principles gleaned from the Supreme Court decisions**. (McCarthy, p. 18, emphasis added)

Prior to the Supreme Court's decision in *Morse*, courts relied almost exclusively on *Fraser* and *Kuhlmeier* in the nineteen years that followed those decisions, and the emphasis was so great that some scholars called into question whether *Tinker* was still even relevant (McCarthy, p. 18). Lower courts have provided an extremely broad interpretation of what constituted a curriculum related or school-sponsored activity because courts recognized "the key consideration is whether the expression is viewed as bearing the school's imprimatur; only under such circumstances is *Hazelwood*'s broad deference to school authorities triggered" (p. 19).

While not frequently used *Tinker* was still a relevant faction of the trilogy and had actually begun to enjoy a slight resurgence, most notably because the Ninth Circuit had decided a recent case based on the *second* prong of *Tinker*. While the material and substantial disruption prong was regularly utilized, the "expression interfered with the rights of others" had "rarely been interpreted" by the courts (p. 22). However, the Ninth Circuit relied on the second and seldom used point from *Tinker* in upholding a school's suppression of a student's t-shirt degrading homosexuality (McCarthy, p. 22; *see also* Canter and Pardo).[25]

---

[25] The case referenced by McCarthy and Canter and Pardo was *Harper v. Poway Unified School Dist.*, (2006). The facts of *Harper* as stated in the Canter and Pardo article:

On the 2004 Day of Silence (an annual student-led event raising awareness of discrimination against homosexuals), Tyler Chase Harper, a sophomore at Poway [High School] and a devout Christian, decided to express his opposition to the Day of Silence. Harper believed that homosexual behavior was "destructive to humankind ... and immoral ... He wore a t-shirt with "I WILL NOT ACCEPT WHAT GOD HAS CONDEMNED" taped on the front, and "HOMOSEXUALITY IS SHAMEFUL" taped on the back, with a biblical citation. Apparently, no one noticed. The next day he changed the t-shirt message to read "BE ASHAMED OUR SCHOOL EMBRACED WHAT GOD HAS CONDEMNED" on the front, and "HOMSEXUALITY [sic] IS SHAMEFUL" on the back, again followed by a biblical citation.

With this new message, Harper got a rise out of his fellow students, and was "confronted by a group of students on campus" that very morning, resulting in a "tense verbal conversation." Soon afterward, his teacher noticed that Harper's t-shirt had "caused a disruption" in the classroom. The teacher thought that Harper's t-shirt "created a negative and hostile working environment for others," and sent Harper to the front office.

Harper may not have realized how seriously administrators would take his t-shirt. Just two hours earlier, a "very upset" man claiming to be a parent had called the school and threatened them for "condoning" the Day of Silence. The caller said that he and others had "had it" and "would be doing something about it." He "said he was coming to campus that day," causing administrators to fear for the safety of the school. The administrators called to get their assigned deputy sheriff on campus as soon as possible. When Harper arrived in the office they thought his situation might be related and were concerned that his t-shirt might incite violence.

The looming decision in *Morse*, sparked hope and anticipation that the Court would use the opportunity to clarify the murky and disjointed approaches taken by the courts in deciding the limitations of student speech and expression rights in school. However this was not the case, the Court developed a fourth standard in its *Morse* holding separate from its previous three decisions. The Court failed to provide meaningful guidance for student speech issues in its *Morse* decision (Canter & Pardo, p. 129). Instead of alleviating the uncertainty surrounding student speech rights in school, the Court added an additional layer to the confusion surrounding not only the extent of students' expression rights but the manner in which the lower courts were interpreting the Supreme Court's decisions.

Not only did *Morse* provide another approach to evaluating the constitutionality of student speech, it was a significant detour from the Courts previous student expression rulings because it opened the door to content regulation of student expression; a practice the Court had avoided in the past (Nairn, 2008). It also articulated and targeted a particular viewpoint – pro-drug speech – that the Court deemed unworthy of First Amendment protection, and further limited student protected expression at school. Nairn concluded that this was a severe

---

Several school officials spoke with Harper. The school's deputy sheriff briefly met with Harper to document the t-shirt and assess the potential for violence. The deputy sheriff warned the school officials that, in his opinion, Harper's t-shirt "could lead to disruption between the students." Assistant Principal Edward Giles chatted with Harper ... He suggested that Harper make the message more "non-confrontational," and encouraged him to become an officer of the Bible Club.

Principal Fisher spoke with Harper about the physical dangers that could result from Harper's t-shirt, and how inflammatory Harper's particular choice of language was to other students, but Harper would not change his t-shirt ... Principal Fisher had Harper remain in the front office, gave him credit for attendance, and did not suspend him or place anything in his disciplinary file. Harper did not display the t-shirt message again, and [principal] Poway did not further discipline Harper. Soon thereafter, Harper filed a complaint alleging that Poway violated his First Amendment right to freedom of speech. (p. 139 – 142, internal citation omitted).

departure from the *Tinker* student expression standard and broadened the gap between protected adult and protected student expression (pp. 247-248).

While Justice Alito's concurrence attempted to limit the reach of the *Morse* decisions, opponents of decision concluded that the Court did not do enough to limit its holding to pro-drug messages or to distinguish drug related language from other dangers facing students (*see* Narin, p. 252). Critics contend that the decision left open the possibility for content regulation and restriction of student speech that advocates harmful rather than only illegal behavior (p. 252), and that the decision would allow schools to restrict legitimate expression on the topic of drugs. Furthermore, the Court's ruling falsely assumed there was a clear line between political and non-political speech, which contributed to the overly broad nature of the decision (p. 253). While these concerns may or may not be legitimate, the standard in *Morse* remains valid and remains the most recent Supreme Court opinion on student speech rights in school.

The Court's conclusion and creation of a new category of unprotected student speech, (i.e., speech that could be reasonably and constitutionally regulated by school officials), generated a fourth principle for determining the constitutionality of certain student speech and expression in school: **School officials may restrict student expression they reasonably believe promotes or advocates illegal drug use in school or at school related activities.** The Court's *Morse* decision utilized portions of the approaches used by the Supreme Court in other cases, but distinguished the facts of those cases and the speech or expression at issue from the circumstances faced by the *Morse* Court (e.g., *Morse*, pp. 2626-2627).

Although *Tinker* expressly articulated students' First Amendment speech and expression rights in school, the Court reduced student speech and expression rights in *Fraser* and *Kuhlmeier*, and had created three different principles for addressing student speech and expression in the process (*Morse*, 2007, pp. 2626-2627). The *Morse* decision added a fourth principle. In his *Morse* concurrence, Justice Thomas referenced Justice Black's *Tinker* dissent, and stated:

> Justice Black may not have been 'a prophet or the son of a prophet' but his dissent in *Tinker* has proved prophetic. In the

name of the First Amendment, *Tinker* has undermined the traditional authority of teachers to maintain order in the public schools. (p. 2636)

Thomas wrote separately in *Morse* to argue that the *Tinker* standard had no constitutional basis, and concluded:

> I join the Court's [*Morse*] opinion because it erodes *Tinker*'s hold in the realm of student speech, even though it does so by adding to the patchwork of exceptions to the *Tinker* standard. I think the better approach is to dispense with *Tinker* altogether, and given the opportunity, I would do so. (p. 2636)

Forty years after *Tinker* was decided, Justice Black's dissent, as well as *Tinker*'s holding, continues to influence the Supreme Court's opinions concerning student speech and expression in school. As Justice Black encouraged, student speech and expression rights have been restricted, but as Justice Thomas pointed out, the approach has been a "patchwork of exceptions" (*Morse*, p. 311), which schools, districts, and courts are forced to navigate in an attempt to limit student speech in school, while respecting the students' Constitutional rights.

PART II.

Beyond Armbands, Bong HiTS, and Assemblies

While the Supreme Court decisions in *Tinker* v. *Des Moines Indep. Sch. Dist.* (1969), *Bethel Sch. Dist.* v. *Fraser* (1986), *Hazelwood Sch. Dist.* v. *Kuhlmeier* (1988), and *Morse* v. *Frederick* (2007) provide the Supreme Court's perspective of student speech and expression in school and offer four principles for guiding the First Amendment analysis of student speech and expression situations, the lower federal court have utilized these decisions to further shape student speech rights in the school setting (*see Palmer* v. *Waxahachie Indep. Sch. Dist.*, 2009, p. 507). The lower courts have applied the decisions and the principles established in the decisions to a variety of circumstances and have addressed an array of challenges faced by school leaders in the context of student speech in school. The lower federal court decisions populate the areas of the student speech and expression spectrum between the Supreme Court's four decisions; however, the decisions are not uniform nor do they address every possible student speech situation.

The Supreme Court's four decisions on student speech and expression in school attempt to strike a balance between respecting students' First Amendment rights and school leaders' responsibility for maintaining a productive educational environment. The Court addressed the facts of four different specific situations, but the decisions for the cases developed principles that have applicability beyond the circumstances that came before the Court. By reviewing and being knowledge of the themes that run through these decisions, school leaders will be in a better place to address the challenges they may face in the future. While not providing all the answers, understanding the decisions that have been made by the courts can provide school leaders additional direction for making informed decisions when confronted with student speech and expression dilemmas in the future.

The four Supreme Court decisions regarding student speech and expression have generated four principles for evaluating student speech and expression in schools.[26] Application of these principles has resulted in varied approaches to student speech and expression issues by lower federal courts. However, each lower federal court decision concerning student speech or expression discussed part 2 includes an interpretation of, or reference to, *Tinker*, *Fraser*, *Kuhlmeier*, or *Morse*, regardless whether the court ruled in favor of the student or the school.

In *Tinker*, the Court established that students retain First Amendment rights when they enter school, although the rights must be examined in light of the special characteristics of the school environment. Student expression may not be suppressed unless "school officials reasonably conclude that it will materially and substantially disrupt the work and discipline of the school" (*Morse*, p. 2626). *Tinker* is best described as governing private, passive, non-disruptive student expression (*Fraser*, p. 680).

In *Fraser*, the Court focused on the manner of Fraser's speech and the ability of a school to regulate speech that is lewd and obscene. The Court articulated that school boards have the authority to decide the manner of speech that is inappropriate in classrooms or school assemblies. *Fraser* posited that schools can regulate speech delivered "in a lewd or vulgar manner as part" of a school program (*Morse*, Alito

---

[26] Lower courts have also utilized arguments outside of the four Supreme Court decisions to regulate student speech in school. Courts have looked at *Morse* for this ability, "Justice Alito … recognized that *Tinker* does not set out the only ground on which in-school student speech mat be regulated" (*Palmer*, p. 508). The courts have utilized a content neutral time-place-manner approach in some circumstances to regulate student speech separate and apart from a *Tinker-Fraser-Kuhlmeier-Morse* analysis (*see e.g. Corales v. Bennett*, 2009). However, the Supreme Court has not articulated any additional principals beyond those stated in its four major student speech decisions (*Palmer*, p. 507) and these remain the focus of Part II.

concurrence, p. 2637). Interpretation of *Kuhlmeier* suggests that schools can "regulate what is in essence the school's own speech; that is, articles that appear in a publication" published or endorsed by the school (*Morse*, p. 2637). This has been expanded include speech that is disseminated under any curricular activity, or published under the auspices of the school, and requires that the suppression be reasonably related to a legitimate pedagogical interest (p. 2637).

In *Morse*, the Court concluded that schools could "restrict student expression that they reasonably regard as promoting illegal drug use" (p. 2629). The majority opinion provided that schools retain the ability to censor speech and expression that takes the viewpoint of endorsing or celebrating drug use, which is expressed at a school event or sponsored activity. The concurring Justices made clear that *Morse* extended no further than speech and expression that endorses or promotes illegal drug use.

It is against the backdrop of these four decisions and announced principles that lower federal courts attempt to delineate the constitutionality of specific students' First Amendment speech and expression acts. The result has been a quagmire of lower court decisions that have taken different approaches in applying the Court's student speech and expression principles. The lower courts' navigation of the four posts of the Supreme Court's student speech and expression jurisprudence has produced varying degrees of interpretation of student rights depending on the specific circumstances confronting the court. Further, the decisions have added depth to the areas of the student speech and expression spectrum that exist among and between the Supreme Court's announced principles, and have further defined such terms as "School-sponsored or curriculum-related activity," and "legitimate pedagogical interest."

Part 2 is broken into nine (9) chapters that address the different types of student speech and expression that the courts have encountered under the broad umbrella of student speech and expression in school. A number of the lower court decisions address categories of student expression that have previously been in front of the Supreme Court. However, in the context of student free speech and expression in school, several issues, including Internet speech and expression and student-athlete speech, have been only addressed by lower federal courts.

CHAPTER 6.

Broadly Defining Co-Curricular and School-Sponsored Activities

The Supreme Court's third major student speech and expression decision, *Kuhlmeier*, provided that schools can regulate student speech and expression that is given in the context of a school-sponsored event or program or published under the auspices of the district. A lower federal court in Florida held that *Kuhlmeier* "controls all expression that (a) bears the imprimatur of the school and (b) occurs in a curricular activity" (*Bannon* v. *Sch. Dist. of Palm Beach County*, 2004, p. 1214). Further, it was established that activities are considered curricular if:

> (1) supervised by faculty members, and (2) designed to impart particular knowledge or skills to student participants and audiences...*Kuhlmeier* never defined curricular activity in terms of whether student participation was required, earned grades or credit, occurred during regular school hours, or did not require a fee. (p. 1214)

This broad definition expanded (and clarified) *Kuhlmeier*'s reach beyond official student newspapers to nearly *any* activity associated with or sponsored by the school, and this position was affirmed by the Supreme Court in *Morse* (p. 2637). Lower courts have agreed on the principles of *Kuhlmeier* and applied them in a variety of curricular situations, yet they have reached varying conclusions concerning the extent of suppression based on different facts facing each court.

Even before the Supreme Court's decision in *Kuhlmeier*, some lower courts were utilizing reasoning that mirrored the eventual *Kuhlmeier* foundation. In *Bell et al.* v. *U-32 Board of Educ. et al.*

(1986), the U.S. District Court for the District of Vermont decided that students' First Amendment rights were not violated when the school administration refused to allow the production of the play, *Runaways*,[27] as the annual spring musical. The school district had funded a significant portion of the production, allowed its name to be used in promoting the play, the performers and crew were high school students, students received grades for participation, and the play was considered part of the curriculum. Thus, the school board "acted within its authority to safeguard the well-being of its students and did not violate [the students'] First Amendment rights in refusing to sponsor *Runaways* as its spring musical" (p. 945).

Although the Supreme Court had not decided *Kuhlmeier* at the time of *Bell*, the District Court for the Eastern District of Missouri had issued its opinion in *Kuhlmeier* v. *Hazelwood Sch. Dist.* (1985), and the *Bell* court cited to and relied on the Missouri federal district court's opinion for guidance. The *Bell* court stated that the play was challenged by the administration because of questions concerning the appropriateness of the school- sponsored play for students of various ages. Further, the school's decision was classified as curriculum-related because the play was considered part of the school curriculum; however, "[t]he distinction between curricular and extra-curricular activities is not particularly pertinent in this context. It is enough that the activity at issue is a school sponsored program" (*Bell*, p. 944, citing *Kuhlmeier* v. *Hazelwood Sch. Dist.*, pp. 1462-1465 [E.D. MO 1985]). As students' First Amendment rights are "somewhat limited, in light of the special circumstances of the school environment,"[28] the court concluded that students' speech and expression rights "must give way to the board's responsibility for the well-being of the larger student body that would be affected by production of the play" (p. 945).

---

[27] *Runaways* "focuses on the emotions and reflections of several child runaways concerning the problems at home, which they fled, and the problems they face alone in the city" (*Bell*, p. 941). The play covers topics including child abuse, child prostitution, alcohol and drug abuse, and rape.

[28] Although included as a precursor to *Kuhlmeier*, the *Bell* opinion also referenced language from *Tinker* in its acknowledgement of the special characteristics of the school.

The year after the Supreme Court's decision in *Kuhlmeier*, the Ninth Circuit, in *Burch et al.* v. *Barker et al.* (1988), invalidated a school policy that required prior review and possible censorship of "all student-written non-school-sponsored materials distributed on school grounds" (p. 1150). Students challenged the policy after the school required the students allow administrators to review an unofficial (or student underground) newspaper prior to publication and distribution. The Ninth Circuit acknowledged that *Kuhlmeier* was the controlling Supreme Court authority, but unlike *Kuhlmeier*, the policy at issue "aimed at curtailing communications among students, communications which no one could associate with school sponsorship or endorsement" (p. 1150). The Ninth Circuit held that the school policy violated students' free speech and expression rights, and applied a *Tinker* analysis. The court determined the policy violated *Tinker* because it allowed the censorship of unobjectionable material not presented to the administration for review prior to distribution and was based on an "undifferentiated fear of disruption" (p. 1150).

The Ninth Circuit concluded that the Supreme Court's decision in *Kuhlmeier* broadly defined "curriculum" and encompassed "school-sponsored publications, theatrical productions, and other expressive activities that students, parents and members of the public might reasonably perceive to bear the imprimatur of the school" (*Burch*, p. 1158, citing *Kuhlmeier*, p. 569). The court reasoned that unofficial or student underground newspapers, like the one at issue in the case, are in "no sense school-sponsored" and are outside the realm of material over which the school can exercise editorial control. Further, there was no justification for a policy that *required* school approval before the distribution of any student written material on school grounds (p. 1158). The court reasoned that "interstudent communication" enriches the education process, and in this situation, the school failed to show that the student publications hindered the education process.

The Ninth Circuit reiterated that student speech, under either *Tinker* or *Fraser*, could not be stifled because of an undifferentiated fear of possible disruption or embarrassment (*Burch*, p. 1158). However, the court clarified that its decision applied only to the content-based pre-approval policy. It did not affect schools' ability to punish students for disruptive conduct after the speech or expression was published. Published only a year after *Kuhlmeier*, the Ninth

Circuit's *Burch* decision began a movement of interpreting the Supreme Court's *Kuhlmeier* opinion as providing a broad definition of what constitutes a "school-sponsored" or "curricular-related activity." However, *Burch* also reiterated that *Kuhlmeier's* applicability was limited to student expression that was actually communicated or disseminated in the course of a school-sponsored publication or activity. Student speech or expression offered outside that context remained subject to *Tinker* or *Fraser* (or now, *Morse*).

In *McCann v. Fort Zumwalt Sch. Dist.* (1999), the U.S. District Court for the Eastern District of Missouri applied *Kuhlmeier* outside the student newspaper context. The court concluded that it could not deem as unreasonable a superintendent's decision to prohibit a school marching band from playing a song that the superintendent concluded advocated drug use. The school took the position that allowing the band to play the song, *White Rabbit*, by Grace Slick, would "send a message inconsistent with the District's strong anti-drug policy" (*McCann*, p. 921).[29]

The court found that marching band performances clearly constitute school-sponsored speech, and *Kuhlmeier* governed such speech controversies. *Kuhlmeier's* broad definition of curriculum-related and school-sponsored activities to reach its conclusion provided the needed rationale for this conclusion, along with the view that school band performances "bore the imprimatur of the high school and the district." Together these findings dictated that *Kuhlmeier,* not *Tinker,* governed the student expression (*McCann*, pp. 923-924).

In addition, the court concluded that the district's interest in not promoting student drug use constituted a legitimate pedagogical interest on the part of the school. The superintendent's belief that allowing the song would send the wrong message to parents, teachers, students, and the community was a reasonable basis for making the decision to prohibit the song. Because the decision was reasonably related to a legitimate pedagogical concern, students' First Amendment rights were not violated (p. 925). Although decided eight years prior,

---

[29] The school leaders believed that the song related or referred to using drugs. He also believed that the band Jefferson Airplane and its lead singer, Grace Slick, were associated with the "drug culture" (p. 921).

the *McCann* holding is in line with the Court's ruling in *Morse*. The Supreme Court provided the same rationale – prohibiting student drug use or endorsement or illegal drug use – as one of the justifications for upholding the school's actions in its *Morse* decision. However, instead of extending *Kuhlmeier* like the district court in *McCann*, the Supreme Court added a fourth component to its student speech in school rubric.

Ten years later, the Ninth Circuit took an approach similar to that of the Missouri District Court when confronted with a question regarding the appropriateness of music for a public high school graduation. Kathryn Nurre, along with the school's Wind Ensemble, wanted to perform an instrumental version of *Ave Maria* as part of the school's graduation ceremony. The superintendent declared that allowing the piece to be played could be considered an endorsement of religion as "the title and meaning of the piece had religious connotations-and would be easily identified as such by attendees merely by the title alone..." (*Nurre v. Whitehead*, 2009, p. 1091). Thus, the Wind Ensemble was not allowed to perform the piece and Nurre subsequently sued the school district and the superintendent.

Along with an Establishment Clause claim under the First Amendment, Nurre pressed a First Amendment freedom of speech claim against the school in that the suppression of the selection violated her right to freedom of speech and expression (p. 1092). As in *McCann* the court articulated that music is in fact speech and subject to the protections of the First Amendment; however, that like any student speech it is subject to the special circumstances and limitations of the school environment (p. 1093-94).

According to the District, the ban was imposed because of the "unique" nature of a graduation ceremony and that the ban was reasonable considering the compulsory nature of the ceremony. In addition, "the district was acting to avoid a repeat of the 2005 controversy by prohibiting any reference to religion at its graduation ceremonies" (p. 1095).[30] Based on these past events and the district's

---

[30] During the 2005 ceremony, a vocal piece of music – *Up Above My Head* – was performed, which contained many religious references. Following the ceremony the school district received numerous complaints from students and parents regarding the religious nature of the ceremony. The local newspaper

arguments, the court limited the question presented to: "when there is a captive audience at a graduation ceremony ... it is reasonable for a school official to prohibit the performance of an obviously religious piece" (p. 1095).[31]

Based on these limited circumstances, the court concluded that Nurre's First Amendment speech rights had not been violated. "[T]he district's actions in keeping all musical performances at graduation 'entirely secular' in nature was reasonable in light of the circumstances surrounding a high school graduation" (p. 1095).[32] While the court found that a violation had not occurred in this situation, the narrow nature of the question and the specific details surrounding the decision suggest that courts could find certain prohibitions against student music selections at graduation (or other events) violate a student's First Amendment free speech rights.

Several students, in their individual capacities and on behalf of a student group, the Lubbock High School Gay Straight Alliance, filed suit against their school and school district, claiming violations of First Amendment free speech and assembly rights and violations of the Equal Access Act after the school denied the group official school recognition and permission to meet on campus (*Caudillo* v. *Lubbock Indep. Sch. Dist.*, 2004). The plaintiffs wished to have the Gay Straight Alliance formally recognized as a student organization, which would allow them to post fliers in the school, use the school's PA system to make announcements, and meet on school grounds like all other student groups. The school district had previously banned "the entire subject matter of sexual activity" and had an abstinence-only sex education

---

also published "letters to the editor" that complained about the religious statements in the ceremony.

[31] The court articulated two caveats to the question: 1. The ceremony was for a finite amount of time, and 2. Providing equal time to every group would be impractical.

[32] Nurre also advanced claims that the school violated the Establishment Clause of the First Amendment and her equal protection rights. The court found that the school district had not encroached on Nurre's rights in either area to an extent that it would constitute a violation of her rights.

policy. The principal, superintendent, and school board denied the group's request. The denial was based on information included on the group's website, links to other websites, and the group's listed goals, which the school deemed to be in violation of the abstinence-only policy. Further, the school believed the information, provided on the group's website, was inappropriate for younger students and was lewd and indecent (*Caudillo*, p. 558).[33]

In analyzing the situation, it was established that the school was a limited public forum, which allowed the school to limit the subject-matter topics discussed on campus, but not the individual viewpoints on the permitted subjects (p. 560). The subject matter restriction was deemed reasonable in light of the educational mission of the school district: "a school need not tolerate student speech that is inconsistent with its basic educational mission" (p. 563, quoting *Kuhlmeier*, p. 266). Ultimately, the court concluded that the school's decision was reasonable and did not violate the students' free speech rights.

The court also explained that the decision was viewpoint neutral because the school would have denied access to any group that violated the school's policy regarding discussion of sexual activity, and "the group was, at its core, based on sexual activity" (*Caudillo*, p. 561). The court stated that it was inappropriate to make the information available to younger students, and that a portion of the information contained on the group's website and the "group's goal of discussing sex" was within the purview of speech and expression that was indecent. Under Supreme Court precedent, the district was found to have the right to

---

[33] The group listed safe sex education as one of its goals. The group's website included links to information such as "New Sexy Gay Game Pics and Favorite Questions...articles on (1) Why Am I Having Erection Problems?; (2) How Safe is Oral Sex?; (3) The Truth About Barebacking; (4) First Time With Anal Sex; (5) Kissing and Mutual Masturbation; (6) How Safe Are Rimming and Fingering?; (7) The Lowdown on Anal Warts." This material was available at the time of the original request, was reviewed by administrators, but removed before the district made the final decision. Content such as How to Use a Condom; Discuss Safer Sex with Your Partner...Unprotected Oral Sex, and Safer Sex: How?" and other sexual materials were still accessible at the time of the district's decision and safe sex remained a stated goal (pp. 557-558).

regulate this type of speech and expression. As the abstinence-only policy was reasonable, the school did not have to tolerate speech and expression that violated the policy. Thus, denying access to the student group was legal in light of the school forum and the group's violation of the abstinence-only policy by encouraging conversations about sex. The decision did not constitute viewpoint discrimination, and did not violate the students' First Amendment speech and expression rights (p. 564).

Boca Raton Community High School in Florida was undergoing substantial renovations and the school administration invited students to paint murals on the temporary construction walls to help beautify the school while the renovations were taking place. Sharah Bannon and other members of the school's Fellowship of Christian Athletes student group decided to participate in the beautification project (*Bannon v. Sch. Dist. of Palm Beach County*, 2004). The school did not specifically inform students that they were prohibited from including religious messages in the murals, but made it clear the murals could not be profane or offensive to anyone. Sharah and her friends painted three murals, all with religious messages. One mural was next to the school's main office, the second only a few wall panels away, and the third was located in the school's main hallway.[34] The following school day, the murals generated a great amount of discussion and controversy among teachers and students and attracted the attention of the local media. In response, the school administration asked Sharah to paint over the "overt religious words and sectarian symbols," however, no disciplinary action was taken against her (p. 1211)[35]

Sharah filed suit claiming that her free expression (and free exercise) rights under the First Amendment had been violated because

---

[34] Mural 1 contained "a crucifix in the background, and paraphrased *John* 3:16 as 'Because He Loved, He Gave.'" The second mural read "Jesus has time for you; do you have time for Him?" The third mural read "God Loves You. What Part of Thou Shalt Not Didn't You Understand? God."

[35] Although the Supreme Court usually refers to students by last name in decisions (*see gen. Tinker; Morse*), the lower federal courts often refer to the student by first name. In reviewing the federal court decisions, the study stayed consistent with the name utilized by the court in a particular decision.

of the removal or modification of the murals. Sharah argued that the expression was private and passive student expression protected under *Tinker*. The school district argued that *Kuhlmeier* was applicable. In reaching the conclusion that the school district could reasonably restrict Sharah's expression and that such restrictions did not violate the First Amendment, the Eleventh Circuit found that the decision in *Kuhlmeier* provided the appropriate framework for analysis.

The court established that murals inside the school, painted by school students, under the direction of school authorities did not create a public forum and constituted school-sponsored expression (*Bannon*, pp. 1213-12144). It was clear that students, parents, and the community members might reasonably believe that the murals were supported and/or endorsed by the school, especially because one mural was located right next to the administration's office and another in the school's main hall (p. 1214). Further, the beautification project was a curriculum-related activity under *Kuhlmeier* because expressive activities are considered curricular if "supervised by faculty members, and designed to impart particular knowledge…to student participants and audiences" (p. 1214). Although Sharah did not paint the murals in a classroom, "Her expression still occurred in the context of a curricular activity" (p. 1214). Further, the school did not participate in content-based censorship of the school-sponsored speech because the suppression was reasonably related to a legitimate pedagogical concern: "avoiding disruption to the school's learning environment." The school's decision related to prohibiting religious messages on the school's walls was reasonably related to a pedagogical concern because it ended the disruption the murals initially caused (p. 1217).

Although the case could be viewed as a dispute concerning student expression, it is also an interpretation of what constitutes curriculum-related activity under *Kuhlmeier*. Sharah believed her expression was private, silent, passive expression (*Tinker* approach) while the school saw it as school-sponsored expression (*Kuhlmeier* rationale). Regardless of a student's intentions with regard to her speech, the circumstances surrounding a student's passive, private expression can transform the speech into school-sponsored expression, subjecting it to greater restriction by school officials. Painting the murals was not an assignment and the students did not receive grades; however, under the definition of curricular-related activity, the speech was determined to be school-sponsored.

Four years later, the Tenth Circuit Court of Appeals encountered a factual situation comparable to the situation encountered by the Eleventh Circuit. In the summer of 1999, after the horrific events that had transpired at Columbine High School during the previous spring, Columbine High School sponsored a project that allowed students and members of the community affected by the shooting to create tiles that would be hung in the halls of the school. Columbine teachers supervised the painting of the tiles, and the school had established guidelines for the project, which required that the tiles could make no reference to "the attack, to the date of the attack, April 20, 1999, or 4/20/93 [sic], no names or initials of students, no Columbine ribbons, no religious symbols, and nothing obscene or offensive" (*Fleming* v. *Jefferson County Sch. Dist.*, 2002, p. 921). Ninety of the approximately 2,100 tiles did not meet the guidelines and were removed from the project. The guidelines were later relaxed to allow people to paint children's' names, initials, dates (other than 4-20), and the Columbine ribbon, but religious symbols, the date of the shooting, and anything obscene or offensive were still prohibited (p. 922).

Parents, students, and other individuals who painted tiles filed suit claiming that the school's restriction on the content of the tiles violated their First Amendment free speech rights. The plaintiffs argued that the expression was private speech governed by the ruling in *Tinker* while the school alleged that the tile project constituted school-sponsored expression governed by *Kuhlmeier*. The Tenth Circuit agreed with the school and concluded that it was school-sponsored expression (p. 923). The court stated:

> Expressive activities that students, parents, and members of the public might reasonably perceive to bear the imprimatur of the school constitute school-sponsored speech, over which the school may exercise editorial control, so long as its actions are reasonably related to legitimate pedagogical concerns. (pp. 923-924)

The court went on to state that this standard was based on the Court's *Kuhlmeier* decision, and explained that "pedagogical concern" means related to learning and can extend beyond academics (p. 925).

However, the court also concluded that under *Kuhlmeier* educators may make viewpoint based decisions about school-sponsored student expression (p. 926). Because of the special characteristics of the school environment, educators needed to be granted this deference. The Tenth Circuit admitted that the U.S. Circuit Courts of Appeals are split on the issue of viewpoint based decisions, but sided with the circuits that had previously held the viewpoint-neutrality was not necessary when a school was controlling school-sponsored expression:

> Given the types of decisions that the *Kuhlmeier* Court recognized face educators in 'awakening the child to cultural values' and promoting conduct consistent with 'the shared values of a civilized social order,' we conclude that *Kuhlmeier* does not require viewpoint neutrality. (pp. 928-929)

Under *Kuhlmeier*, the project was not an open forum and the school maintained control of the project from beginning to end (p. 929) because by affirmatively retaining editorial control, the school refrained from opening the project for indiscriminate use and participation. The individual tiles – created by students and community members – were also school-sponsored. They were affixed to the walls of the school, which showcased the school's approval of each tile. The fact that the school organized the project, oversaw the completion of the tiles, and mounted them on the school walls could reasonable convey a message of the school's approval of the content. Thus, the tiles bore the imprimatur of the school (p. 931). The project also had a legitimate pedagogical interest, which was helping beautify the school after the shooting. Further, the school wanted to avoid any entanglement or disruption by affixing religious messages to the school's walls. The restrictions were imposed in a school-sponsored activity and were reasonably related to these pedagogical interests. Thus, the restrictions did not violate the plaintiffs' First Amendment rights.

The courts do not always side with the school district; there are circumstances where the school has gone too far in limiting student speech or expression and the court sides with the Student. Betsy

Hansen was one of those students. Betsy was a student at Ann Arbor Pioneer High School. She was a member of "Pioneers for Christ," (PFC) the school's Christian student club and wanted to be involved in the school's diversity week. Diversity Week activities included a panel discussion on religion and homosexuality organized by the school's Gay/Straight Alliance Club (GSA). Instead of having students sit on the panel, the panel consisted of adult religious leaders from Ann Arbor. Betsy desired to have the PFC viewpoint represented on the panel; however, her request was denied, and the panel took place with "six pro-homosexual adult clergy and religious leaders...None of the clergy...was Roman Catholic nor shared the Roman Catholic beliefs regarding homosexuality" (*Hansen v. Martin*, 2003, pp. 789-791).

In an attempt to placate Betsy, because of her exclusion from the panel, the school offered to let her speak at the school's general assembly. School administrators, however, objected to a portion of her speech because it "targeted an individual group, specifically homosexuals," and Betsy was ordered to change the speech (*Hansen,* pp. 791-792).[36] As a result of these events, Betsy filed suit claiming that the school violated her First Amendment free speech rights.

Kuhlmeier rationale was applied to both situations because the panel and the assembly constituted school-sponsored activities, but reiterated that even under *Kuhlmeier,* "A school's restrictions on speech reasonably related to legitimate pedagogical concerns must still be viewpoint-neutral" (*Hansen,* p. 796). The court found that the school's restrictions and actions were not viewpoint neutral and "were predominantly motivated by their disagreement with Betsy's and the

---

[36] The objectionable portion of the speech read: One thing I don't like about Diversity Week is the way that racial diversity, religious diversity, and sexual diversity are lumped together and compared as if they are the same things. Race is not strictly an idea. It is something you are born with; something that doesn't change throughout your life, unless your [sic] Michael Jackson, but that's a special case. It involves no choice or action. On the other hand, your religion is your choice. Sexuality implies an action, and there are people who have been straight, then gay, then straight again. I completely and whole-heartedly support racial diversity, but I can't accept religious and sexual ideas or actions that are wrong" (pp. 791-792).

PFC's message" (p. 800). The school made Betsy change her speech because she stated that she could not accept "sexual orientation or religious teachings that she believes are wrong" (p. 800), and that her exclusion (and PFC's) from the panel was motivated by similar concerns. The court cited numerous examples and quoted a statement from the GSA advisor, which was published in the student newspaper, as evidence of the suppression being based on disagreement with Betsy's viewpoint (p. 800).[37]

It was Betsy's viewpoint, not a pedagogical concern, that drove the administration's decision to exclude her participation. "That defendants can say...they were advancing the goal of promoting acceptance and tolerance for minority points of view by their demonstrated *in*tolerance for a viewpoint that was not consistent with their own is hardly worthy of serious comment" (*Hansen*, pp. 801-802, emphasis in original). The school's concerns were not based on pedagogical concerns but political, cultural, or religious concerns, none of which constituted a legitimate basis for restricting Hansen's speech. "The record is quite clear that Defendants' motivation was precisely the opposite [of viewpoint neutral]: to ensure that only one viewpoint was presented by the panel" (p. 803). U.S. District Court for the Eastern District of Michigan concluded that Betsy's free speech rights were violated because the school prohibited her from giving her "what diversity means to me" speech and excluded her viewpoint from the homosexuality and religion panel during the school's diversity week programming.

The *Hansen* court took the opposite side of the viewpoint neutrality argument from the *Fleming* court. This dichotomy illustrates lower courts' disagreement over certain nuances contained in the Supreme Court's student speech and expression principles. As the Tenth Circuit articulated in *Fleming*, the circuit courts are split on

---

[37] The advisor stated in the paper, "allowing adults hostile to homosexuality on the panel would be like inviting white supremacists on a race panel" (p. 800). It is ironic that the GSA advisor would use the race example because it would more than likely also be unconstitutional to exclude a white supremacist from a panel on race issues for many of the same reasons that Betsy's exclusion was unconstitutional.

whether *Kuhlmeier* requires viewpoint neutrality when suppressing student speech and expression (*Fleming*, pp. 926-927). Without Supreme Court clarification on the issue, educational leaders' ability to make viewpoint-based decisions concerning curricular-related or school-sponsored speech or expression hinges on the location of the school because certain court circuits have found the practice constitutional while others have viewed it as a violation of students' First Amendment rights . A school in Colorado may be able to censor school-sponsored student expression based on the expressed viewpoint, while a school in Michigan would not have the same ability.

Erica Corder and fourteen classmates were named valedictorians of the 2006 graduating class at Lewis Parker High School in Colorado. Each valedictorian was allowed to give a short speech as part of the school's graduation ceremony. However, the students were required to present the speech to the school principal for review prior to the ceremony to ensure that the speech complied with the school's policy governing student expression.[38] Erica presented her speech to the principal and at that time it did not contain any religious connotation or mention her faith or Jesus. However, at the graduation ceremony Erica offered the following remarks:

> Throughout these lessons our teachers, parents, and let's not forget our peers have supported and encouraged us along the way. Thank you all for the past four amazing years. Because of your love and devotion to our success, we have all learned how to endure change and remain strong individuals. We are all capable of standing firm and expressing our own beliefs, which is why I need to tell you about someone who loves you more than you could ever imagine. He died for you on a cross over 2,000 years ago, yet was resurrected and is living today in heaven. His name is Jesus Christ. If you don't already know

---

[38] The student expression policy made no specific reference to religious speech, but did "prohibit a variety of types of speech such as slander and profanity as well as speech that tends to create hostility or otherwise disrupt the orderly operation of the educational process" (*Corder* v. *Lewis Palmer Sch. Dist.*, 2008, p. 1241).

Him personally I encourage you to find out more about the sacrifice He made for you so that you now have the opportunity to live in eternity with Him. And we also encourage you, now that we are all ready to encounter the biggest change in our lives thus far, the transition from childhood to adulthood, to leave Lewis-Palmer with confidence and integrity. Congratulations class of 2006. (*Corder* v. *Lewis Palmer Sch. Dist.*, 2008, p. 1241)

At the end of the ceremony, Erica was escorted to the assistant principal and was informed that she would not receive her diploma until she met with the principal.

At her meeting, Erica was ordered to issue a written public apology before she received her diploma. In the apology, she did not apologize for the content of the speech but for making the religious comments without the principal's prior approval.[39] Erica wrote the statement, received her diploma, and the statement was distributed via email to students. Erica filed suit claiming that her First Amendment rights had been violated in that her speech had been suppressed and that she had been forced to participate in compelled speech through the apology.

The U.S. District Court for the District of Colorado decided these issues in *Corder*. The school district argued that Erica's First Amendment rights were not violated as the graduation speech constituted school-sponsored expression and was governed by *Kuhlmeier*, while Erica argued that her speech was purely private speech governed by *Tinker*. The Colorado federal district court

---

[39] The apology stated: "At graduation I know some of you may have been offended by what I said during the valedictorian speech. I did not intend to offend anyone. I also want to make it clear that Mr. Brewer did not condone nor was he aware of my plans before giving the speech. I'm sorry I didn't share my plans with Mr. Brewer or the other valedictorians ahead of time. The valedictorians were not aware of what I was going to say. These were my personal beliefs and may not necessarily reflect the beliefs of the other valedictorians or the school staff." The principal required Erica to add one sentence: "I realize that, had I asked ahead of time, I would not have been allowed to say what I did" (*Corder*, p. 1241).

concluded that a valedictorian speech is school-sponsored speech. The school had limited who could speak at graduation and screened the speeches before they were given during the ceremony (p. 1245). Thus, the school had not transformed the school setting into a public forum, opened graduation for indiscriminate use, or given up control of the students' expression. In addition, a graduation ceremony clearly bears the "imprimatur of the school." Thus, the school leaders could reasonably regulate the content of the graduation speeches (p. 1245).

Furthermore and as is required by *Kuhlmeier*, that there was a clear legitimate pedagogical interest imbedded in the graduation ceremony. The school offered that the ceremony is a final lesson for graduating seniors and that eliminating or limiting religion from the ceremony serves the school's pedagogical interest of maintaining a position of neutrality with regard to political and religious issues (p. 1245). The court deemed this reason to be legitimate, and that Erica's rights were not violated when the school screened her speech. Further, Erica's evasion of the principal's screening of the speech provided "legitimate justification to require an apology" (p. 1245).

In addition, the principal's requirement of Erica to issue a written apology was determined not constitute compelled speech. Erica specifically stated that she was not apologizing for the content of the speech only that the comments were given in contradiction to the principal's requirement that the speech be screened and approved prior to the graduation ceremony. Thus, Erica was not coerced to adopt a specific belief; rather, she was only required to apologize for ignoring the principal's instructions, and forcing her to offer such an apology was within the school's authority and did not constitute coerced speech (p. 1246). The school district appealed the decision, but the Tenth Circuit upheld the district court's decision (*see Corder v. Lewis Palmer School District*, 2009).

The preceding decisions mainly focus on the breadth of *Kuhlmeier*; however, this limited view of the *Kuhlmeier* ratioale shortchanges its applicability in the school context. These decisions establish that school-sponsored and curriculum-related activities are broadly interpreted by the courts, and extend *Kuhlmeier*'s reach beyond the school newspaper setting originally addressed by the Supreme Court. An activity does not necessarily have to be offered as part of the school's curriculum for student speech and expression offered in the course of said activity to be considered school-sponsored. The decisions also begin to reveal that a single Supreme Court principle cannot be applied in a vacuum, as *Tinker* and *Fraser* were also influential in certain decisions. Further, the different interpretations utilized by the lower federal courts become noticeable. One of the largest differences was the question regarding whether the *Kuhlmeier* decision requires viewpoint neutrality when suppressing student speech and expression that is considered school-sponsored (*Compare Hanson* and *Fleming*). *Kuhlmeier*'s influence, as well as *Tinker* and *Fraser*'s influence, is discussed when considering the distribution of student-created or endorsed materials, student speech in the classroom, and student campaigns and elections. However, as is clear from these decisions, *Kuhlmeier* may be utilized for student expression associated with the marching band (*McCann*), school plays (*Bell*), school beautification projects (*Bannon*), school programs (*Hansen*), and graduation ceremonies (*Corder*), as well as the school newspaper context originally discussed by the *Kuhlmeier* court.

CHAPTER 7.

Distribution of Student-Published or Promoted Materials

Although the publishing of non-curricular student newspapers, pamphlets, fliers, and other materials has led to disputes over the realm of student speech and expression rights in school, the *distribution* of these non-curricular or school-related student produced publications or materials on school grounds has also raised questions concerning the extent of students' free speech and expression rights. The Eighth Circuit Court of Appeals addressed the issue of distribution of student produced publications on high school campuses shortly after it published its *Kuhlmeier* opinion (8th Cir., 1987) but prior to the Supreme Court's issuance of its *Kuhlmeier* decision (1988). In 1987, in *Bystrom et al.* v. *Fridley High Sch. et al.*, the Eighth Circuit held that on its face, a school policy regarding prior approval of student publications was constitutional. The policy provided school administrators the right of prior review for any publication or material published by students, rather than the school, that was to be distributed on school property. The school reserved the right to prohibit the distribution if the publication did not comply with the district's "Distribution of Unofficial Written Material on School Premises" policy.[40]

---

[40] The court upheld the constitutionally of all sections of the policy except section (E), which prohibited the dispersal of publications that invaded the privacy of others, because it was overly vague. The rule prohibited the publication of materials that were obscene to minors, libelous, indecent or

Although the Eighth Circuit had just ruled in *Kuhlmeier* (8th Cir., 1987), which concerned school-sponsored publications, the Eighth Circuit relied more on *Tinker* and *Fraser* in *Bystrom* because the publication at issue was an underground newspaper, which was not school-sponsored. Accordingly, the limited issue was "distribution on school property...The school district asserts no authority to govern or punish what students say, write or publish to each other or to the public at any location outside the school building and grounds" (Bystrom, p. 750).[41] Further, the distribution policy applied to minors, not adults; the policy was in place to "preserve some trace of calm on school property." It was an expression of legitimate community interest in promoting certain moral and social values (p. 751). As such, the policy was upheld, allowing prior review because it was not actually suppressing what the students were expressing and because the court was bound by precedent that prior restraint was constitutional.

After confirming the validity of each portion of the student publication distribution policy, the Eighth Court reminded the school district that under *Tinker,* it was not allowed to suppress student speech and expression simply because it disagreed with the speech, and that *Fraser* required that any penalties be unrelated to the political viewpoint expressed by the students. Further, the Court reiterated that it

---

vulgar, promoted illegal activity or products, constituted fighting words, or would likely create a materially disruption (p. 755).

[41] Although the Eighth Circuit relied on its *Hazelwood* opinion for the notion that prior restraint of an official school message was not *per se* unconstitutional, in *Bystrom* it parted ways with what it held in *Hazelwood*. In *Hazelwood* (8th Cir., 1987) the Eighth Circuit found that *Spectrum* was an open forum and that the school could not censor the content except in very limited circumstances (*Hazelwood*, p. 1374, 8th Cir.). The Eighth Circuit held that the school had violated the students' First Amendment rights. The Supreme Court published its *Hazelwood* decision (1988) six months after *Bystrom* and reversed the Eight Circuit in *Hazelwood*. In the decision, the Supreme Court affirmed a number of the findings and some of the rationale utilized by the Eastern District of Missouri District Court when it decided *Hazelwood*.

was not upholding the wisdom of the student publication distribution policy, only the policy's Constitutionality (*Bystrom*, p. 755).[42]

Michael, An eighth-grade student at Jefferson Middle School in Michigan, wanted to participate in the 3rd Annual Pro-Life Day of Silent Solidarity, held in October 2006, by wearing a sweatshirt that stated, "Pray to End Abortion," wearing red armbands, tape over his mouth, and distributing leaflets containing information concerning abortion and abortion statistics while at school (*M.A.L.* v. *Kinsland*, 2008). During the day of the protest, Michael was told to remove the tape from his mouth and turn his sweatshirt inside out, and that he must stop distributing the leaflets because they had not been pre-approved by administration (*M.A.L.*, p. 844). No further disciplinary action was taken against Michael during the October Pro-Life Day.

Prior to a similar national pro-life recognition day scheduled for January 2007 during the following school year, Michael filed suit seeking to enjoin the school from limiting his speech and expression during the protest. Before the day of the protest, Michael and the school compromised and struck a deal that allowed him to wear a sweatshirt with the phrase "Pray to End Abortion" and red tape on his wrists, but he could not wear tape over his mouth. The parties failed to reach resolution on the distribution of the leaflets.

The school had a student distribution policy that stated, in part, that "any literature which a student wishes to distribute...will first be submitted to the principal...for approval," and gave the principal the right to deny approval if it was determined that the literature to be distributed:

> Would cause a substantial disruption of or a material interference with the normal operation of the school or school

---

[42] Comparing *Bystrom* and the Ninth Circuit's decision in *Burch*, the Eighth Circuit and Ninth Circuit looked at similar prior restraint policies, with relation to underground newspapers. The Eighth Circuit, six months before the Supreme Court's decision in *Hazelwood*, held the policy constitutional. The Ninth Circuit, six months after *Hazelwood*, held the policy it reviewed unconstitutional. However, both courts looked to *Tinker* and *Fraser* for justification to support their conclusions and still reached different results.

activities. b. Is potentially offensive to a substantial portion of the school community due to the depiction or description of sexual conduct, violence, morbidity or the use of language which is profane or obscene which is inappropriate for the school environment as judged by the standards of the school community. c. Is libelous or violates the rights of privacy of any person. d. Is false or misleading or misrepresents facts. e. Is demeaning to any race, religion, sex, or ethnic group. f. Encourages violation of local, state or federal law. (*M.A.L.*, p. 845)

Michael failed to provide copies of the proposed leaflets or seek official permission to distribute the leaflets, prior to the day of the protest. However, the school offered to allow him to post the material on bulletin boards in the hallways and to distribute the leaflets in the cafeteria during lunch (p. 845). Michael rejected the offer and argued that under *Tinker,* the school could only impose this type of time, place, manner restriction on his expression if the leaflets were likely to cause a materially and substantial disruption (p. 846). The school countered by arguing that it could impose time, place, manner restrictions under the distribution policy and that *Tinker* did not apply.

In addressing this dispute, the Sixth Circuit Court of Appeals began by reiterating that America's public school areas such as hallways and cafeterias are nonpublic forums and allow for school leaders to exert a certain amount of control over student expression, depending on the type of expression (*M.A.L.*, pp. 846-847). For the hallways to transform from nonpublic to public forum status, the school must take action that affirmatively opens the forum for public use. "Jefferson school authorities have done nothing to indicate that the...hallways have been opened for indiscriminate use by the public, and the hallways therefore constitute a nonpublic forum" (p. 847).

The Sixth Circuit then concluded that the school's action in curtailing Michael's distribution was reasonable because it allowed Michael to post the information on bulletin boards and distribute the material during lunch in the cafeteria, even though he never sought permission as required by the distribution policy. Further, there was no evidence to suggest that the school's proposed time, place, manner, regulation of Michael's speech was based on a desire to suppress his anti-abortion viewpoint (*M.A.L.*, p. 847). Furthermore, it was reasonable for the school to require prior approval of student literature proposed for distribution as the policy was viewpoint neutral and provided guidelines for school leaders to follow when making determinations (p. 848).

Contrary to Michael's argument, *Tinker* did not govern the situation because unlike the facts in *Tinker*, Michael's school only wanted to regulate the time, place, and manner of his distribution rather than suppress the expression because of disagreement with the students' viewpoint (*M.A.L.*, p. 849). The court reasoned that schools only need to meet the higher *Tinker* standard when "they seek to foreclose particular viewpoints [rather] than when they seek merely to impose content-neutral and viewpoint-neutral regulations of the time, place, and manner of student speech" (p. 850). Further, none of the Supreme Court's student expression decisions "control viewpoint-neutral time, place and manner restrictions" (p. 850).

This creates an interesting situation for school leaders because it adds an additional step when determining the constitutionality of student expression. Under the Sixth Circuit analysis, a school leader could determine that the student expression falls under *Tinker* because it is not lewd and did not bare the imperator of the school (McCarthy, 2007). However, the school leaders could still have an opportunity to regulate the expression. The school cannot prohibit the speech or expression, if protected speech, but could reasonably impose time, place, and manner restrictions on the expression or distribution of the expressive materials if such restrictions were content and viewpoint neutral (*see generally Morgan v. Plano Indep. Sch. Dist.* Holding that a time-place-manner standard, not *Tinker's* substantial disruption provided the appropriate analytical vehicle for addressing a school's distribution policy (2009)).

Although not always stating them as time, place, and manner restrictions, other federal courts have reached similar conclusions regarding the regulation of the distribution of student publications rather than the suppression of student speech. In *Harless* v. *Darr* (1996), the District Court for the Southern District of Indiana considered whether the restriction of an elementary student's distribution of religious tracts violated the student's First Amendment free speech rights. Bryan Harless was a first-grader who had been distributing religious literature to classmates in the classroom as students were preparing to go to lunch. When the teacher discovered that Bryan was passing out the leaflets, she asked the students to return the literature to Bryan and told him that he could no longer pass out the religious material because it violated school policy. After Bryan passed out similar literature a second time, the principal "called Bryan into her office and spoke with him about other ways in which he could witness [at school] other than passing out Christian tracts" (*Harless*, p. 1342). Soon after the second incident, Bryan's parents filed suit on his behalf claiming that prohibiting him from distributing the religious materials violated his free speech rights. After filing the complaint, Bryan again distributed religious tracts; this time on the school bus. Although the principal again talked to him about the conduct, Bryan was never disciplined for handing out the religious literature.

The school had a policy in place that required a student who wished to distribute literature at school (more than 10 copies) to notify the principal at least 48 hours in advance of the distribution and provide a copy of the literature. The district court phrased the question facing it as "whether Franklin [Elementary School]'s current policy regulating distribution in its schools is an unconstitutional prior restraint" (*Harless*, p. 1353). The court found that the policy on its face did not give the school censorship power for content-related reasons. A student simply had to give notification of what he wished to distribute. Further, the court found that the policy did not require students to wait for approval before distributing information to other students. "Thus, the court concluded that the policy requiring students to submit a copy of the literature to be distributed does not constitute an impermissible prior restraint" (pp. 1353-1354). The policy did not violate Bryan's free speech rights because it did not prohibit distribution; it only required the school be notified before the distribution occurred.

Seven years later in *Walz* v. *Egg Harbor Twp. Board of Educ.* (2003), the Third Circuit Court of Appeals also examined whether an elementary school student had a First Amendment free speech right to distribute materials related to "an unsolicited religious message during an organized classroom activity." For three consecutive years, Daniel Walz attempted to distribute gifts to his classmates that contained or were attached to notes that contained religious messages. During his pre-kindergarten year, Daniel attempted to distributed pencils imprinted with the message "Jesus (heart symbol) The Little Children." Daniel's teacher noticed the imprint and confiscated the pencils. The principal and superintendent later determined that the pencils could not be distributed because of the potential for students and parents to perceive that the school endorsed the religious message (p. 274). At the winter party during Daniel's kindergarten year, he attempted to distribute candy canes with a religious story attached.[43] Daniel was informed that he *could* distribute the candy canes, with the attached story, but only before or after school or during recess, and not during the party. The following year, Daniel again attempted to distribute the candy canes with the same attached story to students in his first grade class during the winter party. School officials prohibited the distribution during the party but allowed him to distribute the candy canes at recess, after school as students walked to the bus, and in the school hallways (p. 274). Following this prohibition on Daniel's distribution, Daniel, through his mother, sued the school district alleging a violation of his First Amendment rights to freedom of expression and free exercise of

---

[43] The story read: A Candymaker in Indiana wanted to make a candy that would be a witness, so he made the Christmas Candy cane. He incorporated several symbols for the birth, ministry, and death of Jesus Christ. He began with a stick of pure white, hard candy. White to symbolize the Virgin Birth and the sinless nature of Jesus, and hard to symbolize the Solid Rock, the foundation of the Church, and firmness of the promises of God. The candymaker made the candy in the form of a "J" to represent the precious name of Jesus, who came to earth as our Savior. It could also represent the staff of the "Good Shepherd" with which He reaches down into the ditches of the world to lift out the fallen lambs who, like all sheep, have gone astray. Thinking that the candy was somewhat plain, the candymaker stained it with red stripes. He used three small stripes to show the stripes of the scouring [sic] Jesus received by which we are healed. The large red stripe was for the blood shed by Christ on the cross so that we could have the promise of eternal life. Unfortunately, the candy became known as a Candy Cane [sic] a meaningless decoration seen at Christmas time. But the meaning is still there for those who 'have eyes to see and ears to hear.' I pray that this symbol will again be used to witness to The Wonder of Jesus and His Great Love that came down at Christmas and remains the ultimate and dominant force in the universe today" (p. 274).

religion. Daniel's claim was based on the school's continual quashing of his distribution of the candy canes with the attached religious story at the classroom winter party.

Although not using a *Fraser* analysis, the court found that the age of students and the context of events are keys in the elementary setting and drive the free speech and expression analysis at that schooling level. In the elementary school setting, "the age of the students bears an important inverse relationship to the degree and kind of control a school may exercise: as a general matter, the younger the students, the more control a school may exercise" (*Walz*, p. 276). Primary grades are not a place for student advocacy, and permitting the promotion of a specific message could undermine the school's "legitimate area of control" (p. 276).

> In an elementary school classroom, the line between school-endorsed speech and merely allowable speech is blurred, not only for the young, impressionable students but also for their parents who trust the school to confine organized activities to legitimate and pedagogically-based goals. (p. 277)

Elementary school students do not have the maturity possessed by high school students to understand that the school does not always endorse or support speech, but merely tolerates it (*Walz*, p. 277). Making the determination of the appropriate boundary should be reserved for the school district rather than the court; "[a]ccordingly, where an elementary school's purpose in restricting student speech within an organized and structured educational activity is reasonably directed towards preserving its educational goals, we will ordinarily defer to the school's judgment" (pp. 277-278).

In the context of a curricular activity, elementary school leaders may restrict student speech that promotes a specific religious message (*Walz*, p. 278). Daniel promoted his religion and distributed symbols of his belief "during classroom activities that had a clearly defined curricular purpose to teach social skills and respect for others…Because of the tender age of the students, the school prohibited the exchange of gifts with…religious undertones that promoted a specific message" (p. 279). The seasonal parties contained an educational component, and the school maintained control of the parties. "It was well within the school's ambit of authority to prevent the distribution" of items promoting a religious message "during the holiday parties" (p. 279). There was no violation of Daniel's constitutional rights when the school prevented him from distributing items containing religious messages during the seasonal parties.

The distribution cases shift the focus from the actual expression to the mode of communicating the message. The decisions demonstrate that *Tinker*'s substantial and material disruption principle plays a role in the distribution situations (*see Heinkel*). However, they also show that regardless of the First Amendment protection afforded student speech and expression, schools may still be able to impose content-neutral time, place, manner restrictions (*see M.A.L.*). This provides educators an additional tool in making informed decisions regarding student speech and expression in school. Further, the decisions highlight that differences exist between high school and elementary school buildings. Comparing *Walz* to *Raker*, it is clear that courts look at the circumstances surrounding the distribution, including the maturity of the student audience, when deciding if a school's restraint of student speech or expression violated a student's First Amendment rights. *Heinkel* also reiterated that age may play a role in determining the appropriateness of the distribution of certain student expression. However, like many other areas of student free speech rights, the particular facts of the situation will likely determine whether the school's or the student's actions are constitutional.

CHAPTER 8.

Classroom and Curricular Activities

The classroom is the teachers laboratory; the location where students are supposed to be taught to levels of deep understanding and student achievement levels raised. While it is the place that teachers most often practice their craft, students continue to assert a variety of free speech and expression violations based on the limits teachers have imposed in the classroom. The Supreme Court and the lower courts have repeatedly stated that the primary mission of the school system includes educating students (*see Settle* v. *Dickson County Sch. Board*, 1995); regardless of this specific purpose of America's school systems, students and parents continue to challenge the restrictions teachers and schools place on students while trying to achieve this legitimate pedagogical purpose.

While students do have a right to receive an education, they do not have a right to place their love of a particular sports team above the teacher's directions. At least, this was the conclusion in *Sonkowsky* v. *Board of Educ. for Indep. Sch. Dist. No. 721 et al.*(2002).[44] The specific question at hand was whether a student's free speech and expression rights were violated when he was not allowed to wear a Green Bay Packer's jersey during a class photo that was part of a class project.

---

[44] Decisions are occasionally assigned page numbers by Lexis. These page numbers are indicated by an asterisk (*) as to not create confusion that the page number correlates to a page number in the appropriate federal reporter.

Rocky Sonkowsky's class was involved in a lesson called GridIron Geography Curriculum, which included a contest involving 400 Minnesota elementary classes. As part of the curriculum, students were supposed to create pictures of a football player in Minnesota Viking's colors (purple and gold) and participate in a class photo and parade wearing Vikings attire or purple and gold. As an avid Packers fan, Rocky created a picture of a football player wearing green and yellow, Packers colors, and attended school wearing a Packers jacket on the day of the parade and a #4 Packers jersey on the day of the class picture.[45] After turning in the picture, Rocky was informed that he had not followed directions and was instructed to color another picture. Rocky acquiesced, but again turned in a picture colored in green and yellow. When the pictures of football players clad in purple and gold were hung on the classroom bulletin board, Rocky's picture was not included (pp.*2-5).

Rocky claimed that the teacher's actions constituted a violation of his First Amendment free speech rights. The court acknowledged that Rocky retained certain rights when he entered the school building but that at the elementary level, his rights may be restricted even more than at the high school level (*Sonkowsky*, 2002, p. *11, citing *Tinker* and *Fraser*). The threshold question was articulated as whether Rocky suffered a deprivation of his constitutional rights because of his love for the Packers. The court concluded that his education had not been affected by the school's actions, his grades were not affected, and he was not expelled or suspended because he was a Packers fan. His rights were not violated when the teacher refused to post his unsatisfactory homework or allow him to wear a Packers Jersey in the class photo or participate in the parade because these events did not significantly affect Rocky's education or a constitutional right (p. *14).[46]

A group of students in the Bethlehem Area School District in Pennsylvania believed the school district's community service graduation requirement violated their First Amendment free speech and

---

[45] Brett Favre wore #4 for the Green Bay Packers for 16 years.

[46] The court acknowledged that a factual dispute existed concerning the reason Rocky did not participate in the parade but stated that regardless if Rocky or the school's position was correct the conclusion did not change.

expression rights (*Steirer et al.* v. *Bethlehem Area Sch. Dist. et al.*, 1992). The district adopted a policy that required every student perform sixty hours of community service between the time he or she started ninth grade and finished twelfth grade. The students received .5 credits for completion of the hours (p. 1340). Although students were free to choose the type of services they wanted to perform, the project had to meet four course objectives.[47] The students asserted that the community service requirement violated their First Amendment free speech because through their actions, they were being forced to declare, "Altruism is a desirable life philosophy" (p. 1346). The district court responded that the Supreme Court had made it clear that community service programs did not fall within the protections of the First Amendment (p. 1346). The court characterized the plaintiffs' claim as "an attempt to place the kernel of expression implicit in all activity within the protection of the First Amendment," but the court reiterated that the Supreme Court had rejected this type of First Amendment argument (outside the school context), which mandated the rejection of plaintiffs' argument (p. 1346).[48] In conclusion, the court characterized the community services as any other educational activity, and held the same place in the curriculum as any other class (p. 1346).

Students in a Wisconsin school claimed that the school's prohibition against showing R-rated movies as part of the curriculum

---

[47] The four course objectives stated: "(1) students will understand their responsibilities as citizens dealing with community issues; (2) students will know that their concern about people and events in the community can have positive effects; (3) students will develop pride in assisting others; and (4) students will provide services to the community without receiving pay." Furthermore the district superintendent articulated several educational purposes of the community service project requirement (p. 1339).

[48] The district court quoted the Supreme Court: "in deciding whether particular conduct possesses sufficient communicative elements to bring the First Amendment into play, we have asked whether an intent to convey a particularized message was present, and [whether] the likelihood was great that the message would be understood by those who viewed it" (p. 1346, quoting *Spence* v. *Washington*, 1974). The court stated it was bound by the Supreme Court precedent.

violated their First Amendment rights (*Borger* v. *Kenosha Unified Sch. Dist. No. 1*, 1995). In considering the issue, the court stated:

> School officials have abundant discretion to construct curriculum, and they only violate the First Amendment when they limit access to materials for the purpose of restricting access to the political ideas or social perspectives discussed in them, when the action is motivated simply by the officials' disapproval of the ideas involved. (pp. 99-100, quoting *Board of Educ.* v. *Pico*, 1982)

The school district had a policy that prohibited the showing of R-rated movies. The court found that not subjecting students "to movies with too much violence, nudity, or 'hard' language" was a viewpoint-neutral, legitimate pedagogical concern and application of the policy. The court concluded that the restriction was a reasonable and constitutional exercise of the school board's authority and did not violate students' rights (p. 101).

Religious freedom has often been mixed with freedom of speech and has played a significant role in defining teachers' ability to limit student speech in the classroom. In *Settle* v. *Dickson County Sch. Board*, the Sixth Circuit decided that a teacher did not violate a student's free speech rights when the teacher prohibited the student from turning in a research paper entitled "The Life of Jesus Christ" (p. 153). The teacher gave the student a zero for refusing to write on a different topic. The teacher (and school) articulated several reasons for rejecting the paper: (a) the student failed to receive permission for the topic, (b) grading a paper on Jesus Christ presented problems because of the student's possible perception that it was criticism of religious belief rather than the quality of the paper, (c) the teacher believed the school didn't deal with personal religion, (d) the student knew a great deal about Jesus Christ and the assignment was to research a topic unfamiliar to the student, (e) the teacher believed the law required that teachers were not supposed to deal with religion in assignments, and (f) the teacher felt that the student would only use one primary source, the Bible, rather than the four required by the assignment. All six reasons were found to fall within the "broad leeway of teachers to determine the nature of curriculum and the grades to be awarded to students" (p.

156). The circuit court stated, "[l]earning is more vital in the classroom than free speech" (*Settle*, pp. 155), and free speech rights of students must be limited in the classroom because effective education depends in part on keeping focused on class assignments (*Settle*, pp. 156). Further, the court stated that it was not the judicial system's place to overrule a teacher's decision that a student should write a paper on a topic other than her own theology. Although the teacher's belief about the law – concerning the interaction between religion and school – might be mistaken, the Sixth Circuit held that it was not the federal court's place to intervene in conflicts concerning the daily operation of schools that do not sharply implicate constitutional concerns (p. 155). The court concluded that it is a teachers' responsibility to "draw lines and make distinctions," and teachers must be given broad discretion to "conduct class based on the content of speech" (p. 156). Thus, the teacher's decision to prohibit the paper fell within her discretion as a teacher, as the decision did not violate the free speech rights retained by the student in the classroom.

As part of a class project in her second grade class, Kelly DeNooyer wanted to show a video of her performing a religious song at her church. Kelly was the "VIP of the week," a program her classroom teacher had been conducting during the school year. Kelly brought the video to school and asked that it be shown as her presentation for the program. The teacher reviewed it privately and concluded that it was inappropriate for her class and for the program. The teacher stated that the video had not been approved as required by district policy and allowing the video frustrated the purpose of the VIP program: developing students' self-confidence and verbal communication skills. Allowing it could establish a bad precedent and she was concerned about the perception of broadcasting the religious message to a room of second-graders. Along with a free exercise claim, Kelly and her mom filed a claim in federal court asserting that the school had violated her First Amendment right to expression (*DeNooyer* v. *Livonia Pub. Sch.*, 1993, pp. *2-5).

Kelly argued that her expression was protected under *Tinker*; however, the Sixth Circuit found that *Kuhlmeier* clearly governed. It was found that the presentation was part of the class curriculum and the classroom was not an open forum; therefore, the teacher (and school) could regulate the content and style of Kelly's presentation (*DeNooyer*,

p. *8). Further, the court believed that the pedagogical aims of the project would be frustrated if students were allowed to present videos. Pedagogical concerns apply not only to the content but also to the medium, which was the showing of a video. Thus, the court concluded that regardless of the content of the video, the concern over the style of the presentation (the use of a video) was sufficient justification for the teacher prohibiting the presentation (p. *9). The court held that the rejection of the video was reasonably related to pedagogical concerns, and the school did not violate Kelly's First Amendment rights.[49]

In a 2008 case, the Sixth Circuit addressed whether an elementary student had a First Amendment expression right to promote his religious beliefs during a school-sponsored curricular activity in a Michigan school (*Curry* v. *Saginaw City Sch. Dist.*, 2008). The curriculum- related event, Classroom City, provided fifth-grade students the opportunity to create a product, market it, and sell (for faux money) the product to other students during a simulated market-style event in the school gym. Joel Curry decided to create and sell Christmas tree ornaments shaped like candy canes with a card attached that explained the candy cane as a symbol of Christianity. Although Joel's teacher, who was overseeing the event, knew Joel was creating and planned to sell candy canes, she had no prior notice that he was going to attach the religious message cards. After discovering the cards were attached, the school administration alerted Joel (and his parents) that he could not sell the items with the attached religious message because the "Classroom City" project constituted instructional time.

Joel claimed that the school's refusal to let him sell the ornaments with the attached religious message was a violation of his free speech. In addressing the claim, the Sixth Circuit determined that *Kuhlmeier* applied to the case because Classroom City was clearly part of the fifth grade curriculum (*Curry*, p. 577). Because the principles of *Kuhlmeier*

---

[49] Other courts have taken similar approaches to the presentation of religious material during "show and tell" type classroom activities. The Third Circuit Court of Appeals determined that a school's decision to prohibit a kindergarten student's mother from reading from the Bible as part of the student's "show and tell" activity did not violate the student's free speech rights (*see Busch v. Marple Newtown Sch. Dist.*, 2009).

apply when the expression is part of a school activity, the court acknowledged that the restriction of Joel's expression had to be reasonably related to a pedagogical concern. The court found that the school's desire to refrain from offending students or parents with the curricular activity and the school's desire to shield young students from unsolicited religious messages qualified as legitimate pedagogical concerns (p. 578). The Court held that the school administrator's decision that the cards should not be sold was reasonably related to an educational purpose and fell within her discretion as an administrator. Thus, there was no violation of Joel's First Amendment free speech and expression rights.

The line of cases addressing student speech and expression in the classroom and curricular activities establishes several points. First, teachers' responsibility to educate students and provide the curriculum directed by the district supersedes students' speech and expression rights. Running parallel to this and concluded by inference, students have a responsibility to learn in the style and manner directed by teachers and the school. Students do not have the freedom to substitute their own judgment or lesson designs for those developed and expressed the by the school and classroom.

The decisions reiterate that *Kuhlmeier*'s mandate that schools can regulate speech and expression that is offered in the course of a school-related or sponsored activity is clearly very broad. The lower federal court decisions embraced the concept that the definition of pedagogical concern extends beyond lessons imbedded in the curriculum (*see Kuhlmeier*, p. 271) and as stated in *Fraser*, can relate to values that the school is trying to inculcate in students or practices from which it is trying to protect them. Further, the decisions concerning elementary classrooms reinforce that courts view the rights of students at the elementary and high school levels differently.[50] These decisions also conform to Justice Black's argument that the federal Constitution does

---

[50] This is exemplified by *Curry* and was addressed previously in *Walz* (*supra*). Although *Walz* was addressed in the context of distribution, the circumstances were very similar and the courts focused, in part, of the age of the students involved in determining that the limitations did not offend the students First Amendment speech and expression rights.

not require teachers and administrators to surrender control of the schools to students (*Tinker*, Black dissent, p. 526).

CHAPTER 9.
Student Campaigns, Elections, Protests and other Political Speech

Political advertising runs the gamut from negative opponent bashing to humorous to strictly factual and in some case to lewd and over the line. While most of these ads are seen on television or heard on the radio, students can often imitate what they see or hear outside the school walls and bring this type of advertising into school elections. While politicians have ample constitutional freedom to express their views in society, students' political latitude cannot always go unchecked. In *Fraser*, the Supreme Court focused on the lewd and obscene nature of Matthew Fraser's speech when determining if the school violated Fraser's First Amendment rights in punishing him for his statements, which he gave during a campaign assembly. Since *Fraser*, the lower federal courts have addressed similar situations concerning constitutionally questionable student speech and expression during school elections and campaigns. Although similarities can be drawn between the lower court cases and *Fraser*, the facts make each individual decision unique and worth exploring.

However, the lower federal courts have often turned to the *Kuhlmeier* rationale over that found in *Fraser* in providing schools greater control over student speech and expression in school campaigns and elections. The courts have based their decisions on the school-sponsored nature of the campaign and the school's legitimate pedagogical interests in holding student elections. Further, the lower courts have distinguished *Fraser*, limiting its applicability to speech that is lewd and vulgar, while the lower federal courts have embraced *Kuhlmeier* as applicable to all circumstances involving speech and expression that can be deemed offered under the auspices of the school.

The fact that Fraser's speech took place in the context of a school election has not influenced lower courts to embrace *Fraser* as the standard for all speech and expression offered in the context of a student election.

The year after the Supreme Court rendered its decision in *Kuhlmeier,* the Sixth Circuit ruled that a school did not violate a student's First Amendment free speech rights when the school deemed Dean Poling ineligible in a student election race because of negative comments he made about the school administration during his campaign speech in a school assembly (*Poling* v. *Ellis Murphy,* 1989). The question was phrased as whether a high school student's "discourteous and rude" comments about the school administration - given during a school-sponsored assembly - are protected by First Amendment free speech rights.[51] Although the Sixth Circuit stated that the question was serious, the court believed the answer was obvious (p. 758).

The Sixth Court reasoned that the Supreme Court had distinguished private student expression that merely occurs on school grounds from student speech that is given in the context of a school-sponsored activity. Speech and expression offered in the context of a

---

[51] Dean's speech read: "Hi, I'm Dean Poling and I'm running for president of the Student Council. It's a common practice of politicians to cut down each other. Instead of doing this, I'm going to cut down you, the audience. Why am I going to do this? Because you idiots are too darn gullible. For example, what is black and blue and wrapped in plastic? A baby in a trash bag, of course. I just made you laugh at something incredibly sick. If I can do this to you, then the administration could probably take advantage of you also. For example, have you noticed that each year there are less and less assemblies? How many of you would like at least a chance at open campus? Would you like a better chance of having the prom in Johnson City? Is there something in this school you would like changed? "The administration plays tricks with your mind and they hope you won't notice. For example, why does Mr. Davidson stutter while he is on the intercom? He doesn't have a speech impediment. If you want to break the iron grip of this school, vote for me for president. I can try to bring back student rights that you have missed and maybe get things that you have always wanted. All you have to do is vote for me, Dean Poling."

school activity is subject to greater control under the *Kuhlmeier* holding (*Poling*, p. 762). As the election assembly was sponsored by the school, the Court found that Dean's speech "was speech sponsored by the school and disseminated under its auspices" (p. 763). Thus, the school could exercise control over the context and style of Dean's speech. His disqualification from the election for comments the school deemed contrary to a legitimate pedagogical concern was reasonable and did not violate his free speech rights.

Adam Henerey applied to run for junior class president, and used "Adam Henerey, The Safe Choice" as his campaign slogan. As required, Adam met with the student council advisor, signed a contract stating he would obey all school rules, understood that all posters and flyers needed to be approved by the administration, and had the school administration review and approve his campaign slogan. On the day of the election, Adam handed out stickers stating his slogan ... which he attached to condoms. He had not informed the administration that he would be distributing condoms with his slogan attached. After being informed of the condom distribution, the principal decided that Adam should be disqualified for failing to abide by the campaign rule requiring administrative approval of distributed materials. Although it is often said cheaters never win, the vote later revealed that Adam had won the election. Adam filed suit claiming that the school had suppressed his First Amendment free speech and expression rights.

In *Henerey* v. *City of St. Charles, Sch. Dist. et al.* (1999), the Eighth Circuit addressed the question of whether in an election, which is a school-sponsored activity and part of the school's curriculum,[52] the school's decision to disqualify Adam was "reasonably related to legitimate pedagogical concerns" (p. 1133). The Eighth Circuit

---

[52] Adam initially argued that the election took place in a public forum, restricting the school's ability to regulate his speech. The circuit court concluded that the school had not opened the election and intended to control student speech, which was evident from the candidates' agreement to abide by school rules, seek prior approval for campaign materials, and that only enrolled students could participate in the election (p. 1133).

reiterated that *Kuhlmeier* provided the appropriate analysis.[53] The point of contention in the case was the constitutionality of the school rule that required prior approval of materials distributed during a campaign. The school asserted that Adam was disqualified for violating the rule while Adam contended that the rule was unconstitutional as a prior constraint on speech (pp. 1133-1134).[54] The court found that the rule furthered the school's legitimate pedagogical interests, specifically "assuring that school hours and school property are devoted primarily to education as embodied in the district's prescribed curriculum, and the interest in preserving some trace of calm on school property" (p. 1134). Based on

---

[53] The circuit court based this conclusion on the finding that the supervision of the election by school officials, the election time parameters established by the school, the requirement that candidates seek pre-approval for materials they wished to distribute, and that the election operated under the "auspice" of the school could lead a reasonable person to conclude that campaign materials were distributed with the approval of the school. Further, the election was held to teach students leadership skills and to experience the democratic process (p. 1133).

[54] The rule at issue, Board Policy KJ-R states: *ADVERTISING IN THE SCHOOLS* (Board Policy KJ-R) 1. *Places* - The distribution of such items may take place in a location approved by principal of the school. .... 3. *Approval* The approval must be obtained the previous day or earlier from the principal or assistant principal. (For materials not readily classifiable or approvable more than one school day should be allowed.) The approved articles will bear the official stamp of the school, "Approved for Distribution or Posting" ... 5. *Unacceptable Items* Hate literature which attacks ethnic, religious or racial groups, other irresponsible publications aimed at encouraging hostility and violence; pornography, obscenity and materials unsuitable for distribution in the schools is unacceptable as well as: a. Materials judged libelous to specific individuals in or out of school b. Materials designed for commercial purposes - to advertise or promote a product or service for sale or rent. c. Materials which are designed to solicit funds unless approved by the superintendent or his assistant d. Materials the principal is convinced would materially disrupt class work or involve substantial disorder or invasion of the rights of others 6. *Acceptable Materials* All materials not proscribed in "Unacceptable items" (pp. 1133-1134).

these findings and applying *Kuhlmeier*, the court concluded that the rule was constitutional because it furthered pedagogical interests. The school acted reasonably in suspending Adam for violating the rule by distributing condoms without prior approval. Although the court held that the school's decision was based on a violation of a school rule, the circuit court also stated that even if Adam's expression had been protected speech, the school still could have had reason to prohibit the expression or punish the behavior after the fact. Because Adam's expressive act of handing out condoms during a school-sponsored student election "carried the implied imprimatur of the school," the school district had the right to separate itself from sensitive topics such as teenage sex (*Henerey*, pp. 1135-1136). Further, the court cited *Poling* for the proposition that legitimate pedagogical interests extend outside the classroom, and that schools have an interest in "teaching the shared values of a civilized social order" (*Henerey*, p. 1135, citing *Poling*, p. 762, quoting *Fraser*, p. 683). The court relied on *Fraser* and *Kuhlmeier* in reaching its conclusion, and held it was within the school district's discretion to disqualify Adam because he distributed condoms, which contradicted a legitimate pedagogical interest of the district, and was done so during the course of a school-sponsored student election (p. 1136).

Like Adam, Mary Philips had been required to sign a list of election rules when she decided to run for seventh grade student council representative. The list included a requirement that campaign posters receive prior principal approval. Mary hung posters in her middle school in Mississippi that stated "He chose Mary...You should too," and in the middle was a reproduction of Duccio's "Madonna and Child." After receiving complaints about the posters and conferring with the superintendent, the principal ordered the posters removed. Mary filed suit and Oxford Separate Municipal School District became a defendant in *Phillips et al.* v. *Oxford Separate Municipal Sch. Dist.* (2003).

The Mississippi Federal District Court hearing the case reviewed *Tinker*, *Fraser*, and *Kuhlmeier* and determined that *Kuhlmeier* applied in the decision because the election was a school-sponsored event and cited the *Poling* decision for this conclusion. The district court acknowledged that *Kuhlmeier* required the announcement of a legitimate pedagogical interest by the school in limiting Mary's speech

(*Phillips*, p. 646). The court found that the school had a legitimate pedagogical interest in responding to complaints that the poster was sacrilegious and that it violated the Establishment Clause. The court held that the removal was reasonable under the facts and did not violate Mary's First Amendment speech and expression rights.

The campaign cases, although resembling the facts of *Fraser* (especially *Poling*) in many respects, reveal that the lower federal courts have routinely interpreted *Kuhlmeier* as controlling student speech and expression in the process of student elections. The elections are seen as school-sponsored events, and *Kuhlmeier* is the appropriate approach for deciding the constitutionality of student speech in school-sponsored expressive activities (*Phillips*, p. 646).[55] The courts have repeatedly held that student elections are not open forums, and in this context school leaders have broad authority to exercise control over the content of students' speech and expression (*Henerey*, p. 1132). The *Poling* court reasoned that educational leaders had this authority because educators have a legitimate pedagogical interest in assuring that participants in the sponsored activity "learn whatever lessons the activity it is designed to teach" (*Poling*, p. 762, quoting *Kuhlmeier*, p. 271). In many respects, the focus of the campaign cases, with the exception of *Poling*, has been about the legitimacy of school rules and the schools' ability to enforce its rules.

Politics enter schools in more ways than campaigns and student council elections. Students also attempt to exercise their free speech rights through protest and other political statements. Student free speech and expression rights came to the Court's attention initially because of the suppression of John Tinker's (and his sister and friend's) silent protest against the United States involvement in Vietnam, which in essence was a political statement. Forty years after *Tinker*, students

---

[55] *Henerey* and *Phillips* both referred to *Poling* for the idea that there is "no doubt" a school election is a school-sponsored event (*Henerey*, p. 1133; *Phillips*; p. 647). *Hazelwood* stated that to be school-sponsored the activity does not need to be conducted in a classroom but will be considered school-sponsored so long as the activity is supervised by a faculty member and "designed to impart particular knowledge or skills to student participants and audiences" (*Hazelwood*, p. 271).

continue to exercise their rights to silent protest and political speech. Schools, students, and courts continue to debate the extent of these rights in the school setting.

In *Chandler* v. *McMinnville Sch. Dist.* (1992), the Ninth Circuit was faced with a situation concerning students' right to wear buttons containing political messages while in school. Following the commencement of a legal teacher strike, two students, David Chandler and Ethan Depweg, entered their high school in Oregon wearing and distributing a variety of buttons supporting the striking teachers. The students' fathers were among the striking teachers (*Chandler*, p. 526). Slogans included on the buttons stated "I'm not listening Scab," "Do Scabs bleed?," "Students United for fair settlement," and "Scab" with a circle drawn around the word and then a diagonal line through "Scab." Chandler and Depweg were called to the office and told by the vice principal to remove the buttons because they were disruptive. The boys replied that they had worn them in their classes and there had been no disruption. The vice principal again ordered the two boys to remove the buttons and they refused, believing the buttons constituted protected speech. The students were suspended for willful disobedience. The students filed suit claiming that their First Amendment rights to free speech and expression had been violated. In addition, they claimed the school violated their First Amendment right to freedom of association because Chandler and Depweg had been singled out for leading the protest.

The Ninth Circuit briefly reviewed the three Supreme Court student speech and expression decisions and determined that *Tinker* was the most applicable because the buttons were not school-sponsored as under *Kuhlmeier* and did not constitute lewd speech as under *Fraser*. The Ninth Circuit specifically stated that in order for the school to suppress Chandler and Depweg's speech under *Tinker*, the school would have to show that facts existed, which reasonably led school officials to "forecast substantial disruption of or material interference with school activities" (*Chandler*, pp. 529-530).

The court found that the "Scab" buttons were not inherently disruptive.[56] Where "political speech is directed against the very individuals who seek to suppress that speech, school officials do not have limitless discretion" (*Chandler*, p. 531). The Circuit Court concluded that the use of the word "Scab" did not establish, as a matter of law, that the buttons could be suppressed and "the passive expression of a viewpoint in the form of a button worn on one's clothing is certainly not in the class of those activities which inherently distract students and break down the regimentation of the classroom" (p. 531, internal citation omitted).[57] Thus, the actions of the school were found to have violated the students' First Amendment free speech and expression rights.

Alex Smith authored and read aloud, at the school lunch table, a three-page commentary critical of his high school's tardy policy. The statement was not only critical of the policy, but also made personal attacks on the school's administrators.[58] As a result of his expression,

---

[56] The school district only challenged the buttons that contained the word "Scab." The Circuit Court found that use of the word was not lewd or inherently offensive. Furthermore, the term had a history of close association with employment strikes and labor disputes, which was applicable in the circumstances of the case.

[57] The court acknowledged that if the school district could show that the "Scab" buttons were a derogatory statement directed specifically at the replacement teachers rather than political expression associated with labor disputes, the conclusion of whether the expression could reasonably lead administrators to forecast disruption might be different.

[58] The district court described the statement: "The commentary stated that the tardy policy was made by a Nazi, and gave the names of some teachers who the plaintiff believed supported the policy, referring to these teachers as "teacher gestapos [*sic*]." The plaintiff devised a crude abbreviation for the tardy policy, calling it "turd. lic.," which he also designated as "turd licking." Aside from criticizing the tardy policy, the commentary discussed the belief that the high school principal, Betty Kirby, had divorced her husband after having an affair with another school principal whom she later married. Mrs. Kirby was referred to as a "skank" and "tramp" to whom people did not want to talk because "no one likes to think about two school principals having sex." The commentary

Alex was charged with "verbal assault" under the school's student conduct code and suspended from school for 10 days *(Smith v. Mount Pleasant Pub. Sch.*, 2003). The issue raised by the circumstance was whether the school district's "verbal assault" policy was unconstitutional and whether Alex's First Amendment free speech rights were violated when he was punished for his commentary on the school's tardy policy.

The court found that both the *Tinker* and *Fraser* holdings applied to the circumstances. Although the comments were lewd and possibly obscene, which would simply require a *Fraser* analysis, the court found they were also related to a political viewpoint (*Smith*, p. 997). In order for the comments to serve as the basis for discipline, the school needed to show that the comments were a substantial disruption to the school's operation or impinged on other students' rights (*Smith*, p. 997). Alex's comments were found to be "disruptive and interfered with discipline" because they attempted to undermine the administration's authority by questioning one administrator's sexuality and announcing another's marital infidelity. In addition, the remarks impinged on the rights of students sitting near Smith's lunch table that complained about having to listen to the rant. The district court concluded that although the "verbal assault" policy was unconstitutionally vague and overbroad, the school district could punish Alex for his "insulting remarks," without the school violating the First Amendment (*Smith*, p. 989).[59]

---

also stated that Assistant Principal Michael Travis was confused about his sexuality" (p. *Smith*, 989).

[59] The policy stated: "Assault: Intimidation of students or staff; the act of verbally, physically, sexually or otherwise threatening the well-being, health, safety, or dignity of persons on school property or going to and from school, including any school activity under Board sponsorship. MINIMUM SUSPENSION OF TEN (10) DAYS. REFERRAL TO THE SUPERINTENDENT/BOARD OF EDUCATION, AND/OR LEGAL AUTHORITIES...*The [School] Board shall...expel a student in grade six or above for up to 180 school days if the student commits a physical assault at school against another student, commits verbal assault against a District employee, volunteer, or contractor or makes a bomb threat directed at a school building, property, or a school-related activity*" (p. 990, emphasis in original).

After increased racial tension and incidents between black and white students at Derby High School and Middle School in Derby, Kansas, the Derby Unified School District adopted a Racial Harassment and Intimidation Policy (*West* v. *Derby Unified Sch. Dist. No. 260*, 2000).[60] Plaintiff T.W. was suspended for three days under the policy after he drew a Confederate flag on a piece of paper during math class, which a classmate showed to the teacher. T.W. was aware of the policy because he had previously reviewed it with a school administrator when he was suspended under the policy for calling a student "blackie" (West, p. 1363). It was undisputed that T.W. did not intend to harass or intimidate any particular student with the drawing. However, the suspension was still justified as T.W. knew of the policy, intentionally violated the policy, and displayed the drawing to classmates, and classmates had warned him that he would be disciplined if he drew the Confederate flag (p. 1364). After being suspended, T.W. filed a complaint alleging that the suspicion violated his right to freedom of expression under the First Amendment and the policy was unconstitutional.

T.W. claimed that the drawing was a peaceful and non-threatening expression. The Tenth Circuit however concluded that the suspicion did not violate T.W.'s First Amendment rights. The court acknowledged T.W.'s expression could be considered protected political speech

---

[60] The policy provided in part: District employees and student(s) shall not racially harass or intimidate another student(s) by name calling, using racial or derogatory slurs, wearing or possession of items depicting or implying racial hatred or prejudice. District employees and *students shall not at school, on school property or at school activities wear or have in their possession any written material, either printed or in their own handwriting, that is racially divisive or creates ill will or hatred.* (*Examples*: clothing, articles, material, publications or *any item that denotes* Ku Klux Klan, Aryan Nation-White Supremacy, Black Power, *Confederate flags* or articles, Neo-Nazi or any other "hate" group. This list is not intended to be all inclusive). Violations of this policy shall result in disciplinary action by school authorities. For students there will be a three day out-of-school suspension for the first offense with a required parent conference prior to readmittance" (*West*, p. 1361, emphasis in original).

outside the school context, but that the Supreme Court had recognized students' rights in school as not co-existent with the rights of people outside the school setting. "A school need not tolerate student speech that is inconsistent with its basic educational mission even though the government could not censor similar speech outside the school" (*West*, p. 1366, citing *Kuhlmeier*, p. 266).

Based on the history of racial tension and past events at the school, it was reasonable for the school to believe that T.W.'s display of the Confederate flag could cause disruption to the education process and interfere with other students' rights. "School officials in Derby had evidence from which they could reasonably conclude that possession and display of Confederate flag images, when unconnected with any legitimate educational purpose, would likely lead to a material and substantial disruption of school discipline" (*West*, p. 1366). It was more than a mere desire on the part of the school district to avoid the discomfort associated with the expression of an unpopular viewpoint. The district had the power and right to act before disruption actually occurred. Enforcement of the policy against T.W. was ruled reasonable and did not violate T.W.'s First Amendment rights.

The circuit court also discussed the policy in terms of general applicability and found that the policy was not overbroad or vague because it was implemented to focus on a particular and legitimate concern. As applied, the "policy permits the administrator to consider whether the student's conduct was willful, whether the student displayed the symbol in some manner," and if the conduct created ill will. Further, the district's interpretation of the policy did not "prohibit the use or possession of such symbols for legitimate educational purposes. These limitations make it likely that the policy will only apply in circumstances where it is constitutional to do so" (*West*, p. 1368).

In *Nuxoll* v. *Indian Prairie Sch. Dist. No. 204* (2008), the Seventh Circuit decided whether a student's free speech rights were violated when he was prohibited from making negative comments at his high school about homosexuality. The day after the Gay/Straight Alliance Club at Neuqua Valley High School sponsored a "Day of Silence," which was held to draw attention to harassment of homosexuals, students at the school, including Alex, participated in a "Day of Truth," which was sponsored by national organizations that oppose homosexuality. As part of the "Day of Truth," students wore shirts that stated "My Day of Silence, Straight Alliance" on the front and "Be Happy, Not Gay" on the back (*Nuxoll*, pp. *3-4). The school banned the students from wearing the "Be Happy, Not Gay" slogan because it violated a school rule that prohibited "derogatory comments, oral or written that refer to race, ethnicity, religion, gender, sexual orientation, or disability. The school deemed 'Be Happy, Not Gay' a derogatory comment on a particular sexual orientation" (p. *4).

The circuit court attempted to strike a balance between Alex Nuxoll's free speech rights, the rights of students that found Alex's speech offensive, and the school's need to maintain order and fulfill its educational mission. The school argued that the rule protected the rights of students that are the subject of the comments. The circuit court recognized that students' First Amendment free speech and expression rights are not unlimited but also acknowledged that the school does not have an unbridled right to prevent speech that it does not agree with or that is critical of other's lifestyles. Further, the court found that there was no evidence that Alex's comments about homosexuality were defamatory or targeted at specific students (*Nuxoll*, p. *10).

The court offered that the school's better argument would have been that the rule "strikes a reasonable balance between the competing interests – free speech and ordered learning" (*Nuxoll*, p. *11). The Seventh Circuit expanded *Morse* beyond viewpoint suppression of illegal drug endorsement speech in developing its conclusion. The court reviewed the Supreme Court student speech and expression decisions, and concluded:

> From *Morse* and *Fraser* we infer that if there is reason to think that a particular type of student speech will lead to a decline in students' test scores, an upsurge in truancy, or other symptoms of a sick school--symptoms therefore of substantial disruption--the school can forbid the speech. The rule challenged by the plaintiff appears to satisfy this test. It seeks to maintain a civilized school environment conducive to learning, and it does so in an even-handed way. It is not as if the school forbade only derogatory comments that refer, say, to religion, a prohibition that would signal a belief that being religious merits special protection. The list of protected characteristics

in the rule appears to cover the full spectrum of highly sensitive personal-identity characteristics. And the ban on derogatory words is general. (pp. *15-16, internal citations omitted)

The court went on to state that the rule prohibited derogatory comments that referenced religion, gender, ethnicity, disability, sexual orientation, or race. The court believed that this was a restriction on expression, but that in the high school context "school authorities have a protective relationship and responsibility to all the students" that allows such a restriction (p. 17). The circuit court held that that the rule was not unconstitutional on its face. As applied, the rule could be unconstitutional because the phrase "derogatory comments" could be stretched to cover too much speech and expression. Applying the rule to the "Be Happy, Not Gay" shirt, the court found that the rule was stretched too far by school officials and the characterization of the slogan as "derogatory or demeaning" was too strong given the fact that there was no evidence of disruption. Thus, the school rule prohibiting derogatory comments was valid, but as it applied to the "Be Happy, Not Gay" shirt, it violated the students' free expression rights (*Nuxoll*, pp. *21-22).[61]

The result of the Seventh Circuit interpretation and application of *Morse* could have much greater implications than the court's specific holding. In discussing *Morse* and its applicability to the facts of the case, the Seventh Circuit acknowledged Justice Alito's concurrence, but watered down his opinion stating, "The concurring Justices [in *Morse*] wanted to emphasize that…the Court was not giving schools carte blanche to regulate student speech" (*Nuxoll*, p. 12). In reality, Justice Alito stated,

> The Court's decision…*goes no further* than to hold that a public school may restrict speech that a reasonable observer

---

[61] The case was only at the preliminary injunction stage and the Circuit Court anticipated that a more complete record would be complied in the future, and that the facts contained therein might change the analysis. At this time, there have been no further published opinions.

would interpret as advocating illegal drug use...I join the opinion of the Court on the understanding that the opinion *does not hold* that the special characteristics of the public school necessarily justify *any other speech restriction.* (*Morse,* p. 2637, emphasis added)

The Alito concurrence was not a mere general statement about schools' ability to limit speech. It was a specific announcement that *Morse* did not create an avenue for schools to participate in viewpoint discrimination that went any further than prohibiting the encouragement or endorsement of illegal drug use.

After acknowledging Justice Alito's statement, the Seventh Circuit did exactly what Justice Alito stated *Morse* did not allow.[62] The Seventh Circuit concluded that a rule, which prohibited a certain viewpoint inside a category of speech, was constitutional and justified because of the special circumstances of the school environment. The dissenting Justices in *Morse* warned that courts could in the future try to extend *Morse* to allow further viewpoint discrimination (pp. 2639, 2645-2646, 2651). Admittedly, in his dissent, Justice Stevens stated, "It might well be appropriate to tolerate some targeted viewpoint discrimination in this [school] unique setting" (p. 2643). However, nothing in the dissent suggested that the Justices would favor a categorical limitation on a broad viewpoint. Justice Stevens went on to state, "It would be a strange constitutional doctrine that would allow the prohibition of only the narrowest category of speech...yet would permit a listener's perceptions to determine which speech deserved constitutional protection" (p. 2647). A reasonable interpretation of the court's opinion suggests that this is exactly what the school policy, upheld by the Seventh Circuit, allowed school officials to do.

In *Morse,* the concurring justices had joined the majority opinion with the specific expression that the decision did not extend viewpoint discrimination beyond illegal drug use and the dissenting justices discussed the complications with participating in selective viewpoint

---

[62] The Seventh Circuit also mentioned there was little of history of disruption at the school based on this type of student commentary, which eliminated a *Tinker* analysis.

discrimination. Only nine months after the *Morse* decision, the Seventh Circuit arguably used *Morse* in a manner a majority of the Supreme Court – the concurring and dissenting Justices in *Morse* – suggested was inappropriate.

Gillman v. *Sch. Board for Holmes County* (2008) presented a federal district court in Florida with a question regarding "whether a public high school may prohibit students from wearing or displaying t-shirts, armbands, stickers, or buttons containing messages and symbols which advocate the acceptance of and fair treatment for persons who are homosexual" (p. 1361). Heather Gillman alleged that the school district deprived her of her First Amendment expression rights and that it participated in viewpoint discrimination when it would not let her wear items advocating acceptance of homosexuality in support of her friend Jane Doe who had been targeted by the principal for being gay. The court agreed.

The Holmes County School Board and principal of Heather's high school banned students from wearing certain buttons, t-shirts, and stickers displaying numerous slogans, including: "Equal, Not Special Rights;" "Gay? Fine By Me;" "Gay Pride" or "GP;" "I Support My Gay Friends;" "I Support Gays;" "God Loves Me Just the Way I Am;" "I'm Straight, But I Vote Pro-Gay;" "I Support Equal Marriage Rights;" "Pro-Gay Marriage;" and "Sexual Orientation is Not a Choice. Religion, However, Is," as well as rainbow and pink triangle symbols (*Gillman*, p. 1362). Heather challenged the ban and the court utilized *Tinker*'s substantial and material disruption standard in making its determination. In considering *Tinker*, the district court pointed out that the Eleventh Circuit had previously "protected the free speech rights of students when such speech was unaccompanied by material and substantial disruption or collision with the rights of other students to be secure and left alone" (p. 1368, internal quotations omitted). However, the court acknowledged that the Eleventh Circuit has upheld the suppression of expression when the student expression caused a material and substantial disruption or collided with other students' rights.

With this standard in mind, the court attacked the actions of the school district for banning the political expression:

The facts in this case are extraordinary. The Holmes County School Board has imposed an outright ban on speech by students that is not vulgar, lewd, obscene, plainly offensive, or violent, but which is pure, political, and expresses tolerance, acceptance, fairness, and support for not only a marginalized group, but more importantly, for a fellow student at Ponce de Leon. The student, Jane Doe, had been victimized by the school principal solely because of her sexual orientation. Principal David Davis responded to Jane Doe's complaints of harassment by other students, not by consoling her, but by shaming her. Davis interrogated Jane about her sexual orientation, informed her parents that she identified as homosexual, warned her to stay away from other students because of her sexual orientation, preached to her that being homosexual was not "right," and ultimately suspended her for expressing her support for herself and for other homosexual students. (p. 1370)[63]

The court stated that if any unrest or disruption had occurred, it had been created by the principal and his mistreatment of Jane Doe and his animosity towards students that supported their homosexual classmates (p. 1371). The school was unable to provide any evidence of disruption created by the wearing of the banned pro-gay rights materials. There had been no threats of violence, students did not skip class or force their beliefs on their classmates. In short, no substantial and material disruption occurred and the school could not have reasonably forecast that such disruption would occur. Further, the expression did not collide with or trample the rights of other students. Thus, the school board was not justified in banning the pro-gay rights expression (p. 1373).

---

[63] Jane Doe was not the plaintiff or even a part to this action; however, the events that she experienced led to increased awareness and support for gay and lesbian students and increased depiction of slogans and "symbols which advocate[d] the acceptance of and fair treatment for persons who are homosexuals" (p. 1361).

The court also found that the ban on the student expression was motivated by the school board's angst about political expression in school. Further, the board's action was promoted and harshly enforced because of the principal's personal bias and disagreement with homosexuality. The unfettered fears and biases of the district's educational leaders did not constitute legitimate grounds for the suppression of the students' speech and expression. The court concluded that the school district's actions constituted a violation of Heather's First Amendment rights and the students should have been allowed to wear slogans and symbols supporting equal treatment of gay and lesbian students.

The student political speech cases can provide factual circumstances that can result in multiple Supreme Court student speech and expression principles coming into conflict. *Tinker* guarantees students the right to private passive expression; however, *Fraser* gives school leaders the ability to suppress lewd and obscene student speech and expression. When a student uses lewd or obscene language in making a political statement, applying a straight forward *Fraser* analysis does not always achieve a constitutional result. As the *Smith* decision illustrated, a student can use lewd and vulgar language in making a political statement, and the court must look to *Tinker* rather than *Fraser* to determine if the speech could be suppressed. Although the speech could be considered lewd and obscene, the political nature of the statement required the school to demonstrate the speech created a substantial and material disruption to justify censoring the political expression (*Smith*, p. 997). Further, *Chandler* points out that when the criticism is pointed at the individuals (school leaders) attempting to quash it, they must be extremely conscious that constitutional suppression requires more than just a mere disagreement with the expression or sense of discomfort because of it (*Chandler*, p. 531). Thus, school leaders have to do more than merely claim that a student uttering an obscene phrase in itself created a material and substantial disruption.

However, a proper analysis could require an additional step involving *Kuhlmeier*. The lower federal courts have concluded that school campaigns and elections fall under the broad umbrella of curricular-related activity governed by *Kuhlmeier* (see *Henerey*, p. 1133; *Phillips*; p. 647). If a student offered the lewd and obscene political speech in the course of a school election, there is a reasonable argument that it could be punished utilizing *Kuhlmeier*, without *Fraser* or *Tinker*, because the election was considered a school-sponsored activity (assuming that the school could establish that it based the punishment on a legitimate pedagogical concern). However, a student could give the same speech in the lunch room and the school would have to show (or reasonably forecast) that the expression created a substantial and material disruption before suppressing it (*see Smith*, p. 997; *see also Tinker*).

The lower federal court student political speech decisions establish that there are limits to student political speech in school, a point the Supreme Court originally made clear in its *Tinker* opinion. However, distinguishing exactly what Supreme Court principle should be applied to determine the constitutionality of the political expression is not always as clear. Simply because a student is making a political statement or protesting a policy does not give the student the right to utilize lewd and obscene speech. At the same time, school leaders cannot automatically prohibit or punish lewd speech if it carries a political message. The circumstances surrounding the speech, whether it was offered in the classroom, the hallway, or in the course of a school-sponsored event, will play a factor in determining if the speech is protected under the First Amendment.

CHAPTER 10.

The Student Athlete and Free Speech

Collisions between students' right to voice opposition to a school's practice or decision and a school district's need to maintain order and control have played out further in the specific context of student athletes' rights. Several courts have addressed student athletes' constitutional rights to speak out against their coaches. In *Pinard* v. *Clatskanie Sch. Dist. 6J* (2006), eight members of a high school varsity basketball team in Clatskanie, Oregon drafted a petition stating that they would no longer play for the current basketball coach because of his abusive nature (pp. 760-761). In addition, the players decided that they would not play in the next game if the coach remained, and ultimately refused to board the bus to the away game. The students claimed they did not board the bus as a show of protest against the coach and to demonstrate their sincerity with regard to the petition. In response to the players signing the petition and refusing to board the bus, the school permanently suspended the players from the team (p. 763).

The players filed suit claiming that the suspension violated their First Amendment free speech rights and that the petition and bus protest were protected expression. The United States Court of Appeals for the Ninth Circuit stated that the petition constituted free speech, but the court did not decide whether the bus protest constituted pure speech because even if the refusal to board the bus was considered protected expression, it was still properly punishable in the school context under *Tinker* (*Pinard*, p. 765). In determining that *Tinker* applied to the situation the Ninth Circuit stated:

The First Amendment protects all student speech that is neither school-sponsored, a true threat nor vulgar, lewd, obscene or plainly offensive unless school officials show 'facts which might reasonably have led [them] to forecast substantial disruption of or material interference with school activities.' (p. 767)

The circuit court concluded that although the petition and complaints were protected speech, regardless if the refusal to board the bus was protected speech, the act "substantially disrupted and materially interfered with a school activity" (*Pinard*, p. 769). Thus, the school did not violate the students' First Amendment rights by permanently suspending them from the team. The disruption had occurred because it was an away game, the school had rented a bus, secured and scheduled the opponent, coordinated and hired officials, and the boycott was an act disrupting an official component of the school's varsity boys' basketball program, which forced the school to either cancel the game or play with replacement players.[64] The Ninth Circuit concluded that this conduct clearly interrupted a school activity and the school's affairs. "Even if we viewed the plaintiffs' boycott as symbolic speech within the First Amendment, school officials could permissibly discipline the players for the disruptive conduct" (*Pinard*, p. 770). Thus, the suspension of the players did not violate their constitutional rights under *Tinker*.

Similar circumstances occurred at Jefferson County High School in Tennessee when the varsity football coach permanently removed several players from the team after the players had drafted a document which stated, "I hate coach Euvard [sic] and I don't want to play for him," and signed the statement (*Lowery et al.* v. *Euverard et al.*, 2007, p. 585). After learning of the petition, Coach Euverard met with each player individually. Student athletes who signed the petition, but apologized were allowed to stay on the team; only athletes who admitted signing the petition and refused to apologize were suspended.

The students, after being removed from the team, filed suit claiming that their First Amendment rights had been violated, as the

---

[64] The school played with replacement student athletes and was beaten soundly.

petition was protected speech and expression. The Sixth Circuit Court of Appeals phrased the question facing it as "what is the proper balance between a student athlete's First Amendment rights and a coach's need to maintain order and discipline" (*Lowery*, p. 587). The circuit court found that *Tinker* governed, and concluded that it was reasonable for the coach to believe that the petition would substantially disrupt the team by eroding the coach's authority and dividing the players. As in *Pinard*, the Sixth Circuit held that the coach and school did not violate the student athletes' First Amendment rights because the potential disruption created by the petition took the students' actions outside the realm of *Tinker's* protections (p. 598).[65] It was not necessary that a disruption actually occur so long as the coach and school could reasonably forecast that the petition would disrupt the team.

Beyond the narrow holding of the case, the Sixth Circuit's analysis of student athletes' rights is relevant to understanding the lower federal courts' interpretation of the Supreme Court's student speech and expression principles and the relation to other Supreme Court student rights' decisions. In reaching its conclusion, the circuit court stated that students do not have a right to participate in extracurricular activities. Pointing to Supreme Court student drug testing decisions, *Brd. of Edu. v. Earls* (2002) and *Vernonia Sch. Dist. v. Acton* (1995), the court reiterated that the Supreme Court had held that student athletes are subject to greater restrictions than the general student body (*Lowery*, p. 589). The court reaffirmed a previous Sixth Circuit decision that stated regulations that could be inappropriate for the entire student body may be appropriate for a voluntary athletic program (p. 597). Further, the circuit court distinguished coaches from classroom teachers. Where the classroom teacher's role is to guide academic development and promote discussion of various student viewpoints, a coach has the responsibility to train student athletes to win on the field. "Plays and

---

[65] The Sixth Circuit distinguished *Pinard*. In *Pinard* the coach had previously told his players that if they did not want to play for him and told him such, he would quit. The Sixth Circuit characterized this as the coach inviting criticism and the coach and school could not later claim that the invited speech created a disruption. Thus, while the student petition was protected by *Tinker* in *Pinard*, the uninvited petition in *Lowery* was not entitled to the same protection.

strategies are seldom up for debate. Execution of the coach's will is paramount," and coaches are entitled to respect from their athletes (pp. 589, 594).[66]

The court drew on the Supreme Court's conclusion that school officials have a duty to maintain discipline and order to support its holding and found that the plaintiffs' actions were an attack on the coach's authority and undermined his ability to lead the team. Further, the petition threatened team unity (*Lowery*, p. 594). By utilizing Supreme Court student Fourth Amendment rights decisions, the circuit court distinguished student athletes' free speech rights from those of the general student body. The court articulated that students do not have broad freedom to question a coach's authority and escape possible reprimand. The circuit court did not say that the students were prohibited from expressing their views of the coach; however, if they chose to express their opinions, it was reasonable for the coach to suspend the athletes from the team because of the negative effect such behavior could have on the team.

The Eighth Circuit referenced *Pinard* and *Wildman* v. *Marshalltown* (2001) in its discussion of student athletes' First Amendment rights. *Wildman* involved a high school basketball player who wrote a letter to her teammates after her coach failed to select her for the varsity girls' basketball team. The letter contained the word "bullshit," which the Eighth Circuit characterized as inappropriate language, and the letter encouraged the players to unite against the coach (p. 772). When the coach learned of the letter, he requested that the student athlete apologize. She refused, and the coach dismissed her from the junior varsity team.

In ruling on these issues in *Wildman*, The Eighth Circuit referred to *Tinker* and *Fraser* and held that the letter and student's actions materially disrupted a school activity (girls' basketball) and removal of the student from the team was reasonable (*Wildman*, p. 772). In reaching this holding, the court recognized a difference between the athletic field and the classroom:

---

[66] The circuit court did acknowledge that there are many reasons students participate in school sports but the most immediate is to win games, and a coach directs students towards this goal.

The school sanction only required an apology. The school did not interfere with Wildman's regular education. A difference exists between being in the classroom, which was not affected here, and playing on an athletic team when the requirement is that the player only apologize to her teammates and her coach for circulating an insubordinate letter. (p. 772)

The Eighth Circuit also noted that coaches are entitled to a certain amount of respect, particularly in the school setting. The court concluded that under the circumstances, the plaintiff's speech amounted to insubordinate speech against the coach and was not entitled to constitutional protection. As in the other circuit court decisions, the Eighth Circuit acknowledged that the coach's decision might not have been the best approach, but under the circumstances, the approach was reasonable.

Although eluded to and used in all of the decisions, *Lowery* specifically acknowledged that the Supreme Court had concluded student athletes have fewer rights in the area of privacy and search, and are subject to greater regulation than the general student body. The circuit courts have utilized this Supreme Court Fourth Amendment analysis and transplanted it to the student speech and expression context. The few available student athlete speech decisions are consistent in differentiating between student athletes' rights and those of the general student body. The courts have articulated distinctions between the classroom and the playing field, as well as the voluntary nature associated with playing sports as compared to the mandatory obligation of attending class. The federal courts have established that student speech and expression, such as letters and petitions, that could constitute protected speech in the general student population, are not afforded the same level of protection in the student athlete setting. These actions, when taken by student athletes, have the potential to create disruption, materially interfere with a school activity, possibly undermine the coach's authority, and divide the team. Further, the courts acknowledged differences between the role of a teacher and a coach and the deference a student athlete must show a coach. As the Sixth Circuit stated, student athletes are subject to greater restrictions, and circuit court decisions provide detailed examples of how schools can limit student athletes' speech and expression rights comparable to the general student population.

CHAPTER 11.

(Not) Saying the Pledge of Allegiance

Although the Supreme Court has heard arguments and rendered decisions in cases concerning state statutes and school policies that require students to salute the flag or say the Pledge of Allegiance ("Pledge"), school districts and states continue to enact such regulations, and students and parents continue to challenge them as being unconstitutional. The Supreme Court addressed a regulation requiring mandatory flag salute in 1943 in *West Virginia State Board of Educ. v. Barnette*. The Supreme Court concluded that compelling students to salute the flag violated students' First Amendment rights (p. 642).[67] The lower federal courts have not wavered from the Supreme Court's holding in *Barnette*.

In *Frazier v. Winn* (2008), Cameron (Cam) Frazier challenged a Florida School District's policy that required students to stand and say the Pledge or required parental permission to obtain exemption. Even if the student received parental permission for exemption from *saying* the Pledge, the statute still required the student to stand during it. Cam was an eleventh-grader who, after being disciplined for failing to stand during

---

[67] In 2004, the Supreme Court heard a case concerning student rights regarding reciting the Pledge; however, the challenge was based on violations of the Establishment Clause and Free Exercise Clause rather than the Free Speech Clause of the First Amendment (*Elk Grove Unified Sch. Dist. v. Newdow*, 2004). Further, the Court did not reach the merits of the case because the Court decided the case on the narrower procedural grounds that the father did not have standing to file suit as his daughter's "next friend."

the Pledge or bringing parental permission for his behavior, filed suit claiming that the school's actions and the Florida statute violated his First Amendment rights.68 Cam specifically alleged that unless the court intervened he would "continue to be subject to verbal abuse or other punishment for the exercise of his First Amendment right of expression by remaining seated" and silent during the Pledge (p. 1281-82).

The Eleventh Circuit Court of Appeals concluded that the Florida statute and the school regulation were clearly unconstitutional in requiring students to stand even if they did not want to participate in the Pledge and violated students' First Amendment free speech and expression rights. The court stated that a student's right to remain seated during the Pledge had been clearly established (p. 1282). The statute and regulation's requirement that students obtain parental permission to be excused from reciting the Pledge, however, was not a violation of the student's rights (*Frazier*, pp. 1282 - 83).

The court approach the statute as a "parental-rights" statute, and that the statute provided students an opportunity to refrain from saying the Pledge but more importantly, "the statute ultimately leaves it to the parent whether a schoolchild will pledge or not" (p. 1284). The court stated, "the State, in restricting the student's freedom of speech, advances the protection of the constitutional rights of parents: an interest which the State may lawfully protect" (p. 1284). While the court agreed that the state cannot usually compel a student to participate in the Pledge, it also recognized that a *parent's* right to interfere with his or her child's wishes is stronger than a school's right to interfere on behalf of the school (p. 1285). The court concluded, "the State's interest in recognizing and protecting the rights of parents on

---

[68] Cam's teachers had excused him from standing for the pledge for several years; however, during a school day that utilized a modified schedule, Cam was in a different classroom than usual during the Pledge. The teacher ordered Cam to stand for the Pledge. When he refused, the teacher told him he had no respect, was un-American and ungrateful, told him he needed parental permission, continued to berate him, and eventually sent him to the office (*Frazier* v. *Alexandre*, 2006, p. 1353-1354). The principal also told Cam that he would have to stand for the Pledge, but that talking to his mother, on the phone, constituted sufficient parental consent for not *saying* the Pledge.

some educational issues is sufficient to justify the restriction of some student freedom of speech. Even if the balance of parental, students, and school rights might favor the rights of a mature high school student in a specific circumstance" (p. 1285).

The Third Circuit in *Circle School* v. *Pappert* (2004) struck a Pennsylvania statute that required parental notification when a student refused to participate in saying the Pledge or salute the flag because it violated students' First Amendment free speech rights (*Circle School*, p. 174). The Third Circuit reasoned that the parental notification would discourage, or *chill*, students exercising their First Amendment right to refrain from participating in the exercises. Further, the notification provision constituted viewpoint discrimination because it was only triggered when students chose *not* to speak (p. 180). The Third Circuit found that the state lacked a compelling interest for the notification provision and as such the provision constituted "significant infringement" on students' free speech rights (p. 181).

The day after a classmate was chastised by his teacher and punished by the principal for failing to say the Pledge of Allegiance, Michael Holloman stood silently with his fist raised while the Pledge was said during his class. Holloman did not disturb other students, touch anyone, or distract his fellow students' view of the flag. The teacher immediately condemned his behavior in front of the class and called his actions disappointing, disrespectful, and inappropriate. The teacher told the school principal of Holloman's actions and Holloman was summoned to the principal's office. Holloman explained that he raised his fist as a protest for what happened to his friend the previous day. The principal punished Holloman by sentencing him to three days detention, stated that Holloman could not receive his diploma until he completed the punishment, and required Holloman to apologize to the class. Due to the short amount of time between the incident and graduation, there was not enough time for Holloman to serve his detentions. The principal offered Holloman a paddling as an alternative punishment; Holloman accepted the paddling as the classroom teacher watched.

Holloman filed suit claiming that his First Amendment rights had been violated because he had been "chastised, threatened, and punished for refusing to say the Pledge of Allegiance." In *Holloman* v. *Harland*, (2008), the Eleventh Circuit Court of Appeals reexamined students' right to abstain from saying the Pledge. The court reiterated that the

Supreme Court has long held that schools may not compel students to say the Pledge (*Holloman*, p. 1268). Further, students have the right to refuse to say the Pledge (p. 1269). The statements appear to be the same argument; however, the court was clarifying that students not only retain a right to be free from compelled speech under the First Amendment but also have an affirmative First Amendment expression right to refrain from saying the Pledge. The Supreme Court has "clearly and specifically established that schoolchildren have the right to refuse to say the Pledge of Allegiance…any reasonable person would know that disciplining Holloman for refusing to recite the pledge impermissibly chills his First Amendment rights" (p. 1269, internal citations and quotations omitted).

Holloman also argued that he had an affirmative right to express himself by raising his fist rather than merely standing silently during the Pledge. The Eleventh Circuit agreed. The court determined that Holloman raising his fist was clearly an expressive message, and stated that the standard was "whether the reasonable person would interpret it [the raised fist] as some sort of message, not whether an observer would necessarily infer a specific message" (p. 1270). The court found that Holloman's raised fist was an expressive message qualifying for First Amendment protection consideration, and that at least some of his classmate's would recognize the specific message – a protest against his classmate's reprimand and punishment the previous day – while others would reasonably see the general message of a protest against the school (p. 1270).

The court explained that under the First Amendment and *Tinker,* a school cannot ignore or suppress expression with which it simply wishes not to contend. The school cannot infringe on a student's First Amendment rights simply because it disagrees with the political message the student is attempting to communicate. The school must show that the expression created a substantial and material disruption of the operation of the school and "more than a brief, easily over-looked, de minimum impact, before it may be curtailed" (p. 1272).[69] In

---

[69] The court noted that this standard allows schools to suppress expression that is lewd and vulgar as it would undermine the school's basic educational mission (p. 1271).

Holloman's situation there had been no real disruption (or reasonable forecast of disruption) and the school's "undifferentiated fear or apprehension" was insufficient to overcome Holloman's expression rights. Likewise, the school could not reasonably allege that the punishment was for insubordination and failure to follow directions (in this case, saying the Pledge and placing the hand over the heart). "School officials may not punish indirectly, through the guise of insubordination, what they may not punish directly" (p. 1276).

Further, Holloman's classmates' disagreement with his political statement was also insufficient grounds for the school punishing his expression. This was true even if the disagreement is disguised as offense or veiled in threats to the speaker (p. 1275). The court reasoned that students cannot be afforded "less constitutional protection simply because their peers might illegally express disagreement through violence instead of reason" (p. 1276). A principal must maintain order of the school, but cannot do so by ignoring right and wrong and punishing a student for exercising a constitutional right because of fear of illegal behavior from the students' peers.

Holloman's affirmative act of raising his fist was entitled to First Amendment protection. He also retained a constitutional right to refrain from reciting the Pledge. His punishment for refusing to participate in the Pledge and raising his fist violated his protected First Amendment rights.

Together, *Circle School*, *Frazier*, and *Holloman* reiterate students' free expression right to refrain from participating in the Pledge or saluting the flag, but as *Frazier* also points out student rights can still be subject to the rights of their parents. Although the decisions do not override *Tinker*'s substantial disruption exception, students may not be forced to stand for the Pledge even if the school suggests that the reason for the standing requirement is simply to show respect. Students have an affirmative right to political expression in school as long as it does not create a substantial and material disruption. As the *Frazier* court stated, "Since *Barnette*, federal courts have established a body of case law that irrefutably recognizes the rights of students to "refrain from participating in the Pledge or saluting the flag" (*Frazier*, p. 1365).

CHAPTER 12

Confederate Flags, Coed Naked, and Heavy Metal Icons: What *Not* to Wear to School

Students choose to express themselves in numerous ways, and their dress if often one of the most notable. As students have utilized dress as a vehicle of expression, school administrators have attempted to limit the dress for a variety of factors. This feud over what students wear to school has resulted in numerous cases being decided with regard to student dress codes. The decisions are split between upholding student attire policies and finding that they violate students' First Amendment free speech and expression rights.

In the Van Wert City School District, school officials told Nicholas Boroff that he could not wear shirts with Marilyn Mason depicted on them to school.[70] A school authority stopped Nicholas during the school day, and when Nicholas was given the choice to turn the shirt inside out, take it off, or go home, he left school for the day. Nicholas wore a different Marilyn Manson t-shirt on each of the next three days and each day he was told that he could not wear the shirt while at

---

[70] Nicholas wore a variety of shirts. The front of the first shirt "depicted a three-faced Jesus, accompanied by the words "See No Truth. Hear No Truth. Speak No Truth." On the back of the shirt, the word "BELIEVE" was spelled out in capital letters, with the letters "LIE" highlighted. Marilyn Manson's name (although not his picture) was displayed prominently on the front of the shirt." Nicholas wore three additional shirts with "pictures of Marilyn Manson, whose appearance can fairly be described as ghoulish and creepy" (p. 467).

school. At the time of Nicholas's shirt incidents, Van Wert High School (in Ohio) had a "dress and grooming" policy in place that stated, "clothing with offensive illustrations, drug, alcohol, or tobacco slogans…are not acceptable" (*Boroff* v. *Van Wert City Board of Educ.* 2000,pp. 466-467).

Nicholas filed suit and alleged that the school violated his First Amendment right to freedom of expression by prohibiting his wearing of the Marilyn Manson shirts. The court established that *Fraser* applied to the situation and found it was a "highly appropriate function" of the school to prohibit vulgar and offensive expression in school (*Boroff,* p. 468). Applying the standard to the case, the court found the school believed the shirts to be offensive because of the bands promotion of "destructive conduct and demoralizing values," which were contrary to the school's educational mission. The band had a pro-drug persona and Manson admitted drug use and promoted its use. The band's mocking of certain religions ran afoul of the school's mission to respect other students' beliefs (pp. 469-470). The court concluded that the school acted reasonably in banning the t-shirts because they promoted values that were patently offensive to the school's educational mission and were deemed vulgar and offensive (p. 470).

The U.S. District Court for the District of Massachusetts reached a similar conclusion concerning t-shirts that offered sexual slogans or referenced male genitalia.[71] In *Pyle* v. *The South Hadley Sch. Committee*, the district court held that a policy that prohibited students from wearing the shirts did not violate the students' First Amendment free speech and expression rights. The court concluded "if a school…administration decides to limit clothing with sexually-provocative slogans…in order to protect students and enhance the educational environment…the court is unlikely to conclude that this action violates the First Amendment" (p. 11).

In a situation concerning expression closer to political speech, a student wore a t-shirt to school displaying a photo of President George W. Bush with the caption "International Terrorist" below the picture.

---

[71] Two shirts were in question; the first stated "Coed Naked Band; Do it to the Rhythm." The other stated, "See Dick Drink See Dick Drive. See Dick Die. Don't be a Dick."

The student stated the shirt was a political expression about President Bush's foreign policy and the Iraq war. Dearborn (Michigan) High School, where the student attended, had a student population at the time that was 31% students of Middle Eastern descent. When the principal saw the student wearing the shirt in the lunchroom, he asked the student to turn the shirt inside out or take it off. When the student refused, the principal sent him to the office where the student called his dad and then the student left for the day. The principal explained that he ordered the student to remove the shirt because it had created a disruption, he was concerned it would create an even greater disruption, and was worried about the student's safety. The principal admitted that the shirt did not violate the student code of conduct and did not promote drugs, alcohol, or terrorism (*Barber* v. *Dearborn Pub. Sch.*, 2003).

In examining plaintiff's claim that the school violated his First Amendment freedom of expression, the court determined that *Tinker* applied because the shirt was not lewd or obscene and it was clearly not school-sponsored or endorsed speech and expression. As such, the school had to show that the t-shirt created a "substantial disruption of or a material interference with school activities or created more than an unsubstantiated fear or apprehension of such disruption or interference" to withstand constitutional scrutiny (*Barber*, p. 856). The reality was that banning the shirt was based on the principal's belief that the t-shirt expressed an unpopular political stance, which equated to little more than a desire to avoid the discomfort associated with an unpopular opinion. This was not sufficient to ban the student's political expression broadcast in the form of a President Bush t-shirt. The court reiterated "maintaining a school community of tolerance includes the tolerance of even the most intolerant or disagreeable viewpoints" (p. 858). The school was unable to show that the t-shirt created a material disruption or was reasonably likely to create such a disturbance, and without this showing the school could not limit the student's right to wear the shirt.

The mascot of the University of Virginia is a Cavalier wielding a saber, and the Albermarle County (Virginia) High School's mascot is a patriot grasping a musket. Across the street from the high school, Albermarle's feeder middle school Jack Jouett Middle had a dress code policy that prohibited the depiction of any guns or weapons or slogans discussing guns or weapons on student attire (*Newsom* v. *Albermarle*

County Sch. Board, 2003). Alan Newsom was a student at Jack Jouett. During his sixth grade year, Alan wore a purple t-shirt to school, "which depicted three black silhouettes of men holding firearms superimposed on the letters 'NRA' positioned above the phrase 'SHOOTING SPORTS CAMP.'" The assistant principal at the school saw Alan and claimed that the depiction reminded her of sharpshooters and the events at Columbine High School. She also thought that Alan's classmates would get the same idea. She had a lengthy conversation with Alan and asked him to remove the shirt. Alan questioned why he needed to remove the shirt and was told the school had a policy that prohibited the promotion of drugs, alcohol, guns and weapons, or the use of any of these products. Alan eventually complied.

During the next year, Alan wore shirts on at least three occasions that referenced the "NRA" but did not depict guns. He was never asked to change these shirts. The middle school dress code policy stated, in part, "students were prohibited from wearing…messages on clothing, jewelry, and personal belongings that relate to drugs, alcohol, tobacco, weapons, violence, sex, vulgarity, or that reflect adversely upon persons because of their race of ethnic group" (*Newsom*, p. 253).

Alan filed suit claiming that the dress code was vague and overbroad, infringing on his First Amendment rights to speech and expression. He argued that the policy was overbroad in that it prohibited even expression related to lawful possession of firearms. The Fourth Circuit Court of Appeals framed the relevant question as: "whether the Jouett Dress Code, which prohibits…messages on clothing…that relate to…weapons is unconstitutionally overbroad on its face because it reaches too much expression that is protected by the First Amendment" (p. 255).

The circuit court initially established that even absent the policy, the middle school could prohibit the display of violent, threatening, lewd, obscene or vulgar images and expression related to weapons; however, nonviolent and non-threatening messages and images related to weapons fall within *Tinker*'s substantial disruption standard. Thus, *Tinker*, not *Fraser* or *Kuhlmeier*, was utilized to determine the constitutionality of the policy (*Newsom*, p. 256). The court also pointed out that the special characteristic of the school environment granted schools more discretion in suppressing student expression:

Courts have recognized that, even though speech codes in general are looked at with disfavor under the First Amendment because of their tendency to silence or interfere with protected speech, a public school's speech/disciplinary policy need not be as detailed as a criminal code ... the demands of public secondary and elementary school discipline are such that it is inappropriate to expect the same level of precision in drafting school disciplinary policies as is expected of legislative bodies crafting criminal restrictions. (p. 258, quoting *Fraser*, p. 686)

Against the backdrop of *Tinker* and the special circumstances of the school environment, the Fourth Circuit evaluated the dress code. The court found that there was no evidence that the clothing that contained messages related to weapons worn by students substantially disrupted or materially interfered with school operations. The court concluded that the dress restriction was not needed to maintain discipline at the school (*Newsom*, p. 259). As such, the school policy could "be understood as reaching lawful, nonviolent, and non-threatening symbols of not only popular, but important organizations and ideals." The circuit court provided several examples of speech, expression, and symbols that would be prohibited under the policy, including the State Seal of Virginia, the University of Virginia insignia (two crossed sabers), and images of the district's high school mascot. Further, under the policy, a student could wear a shirt that read "No War" but neither a shirt that depicted American troops sitting atop a tank with the message "Support our Troops" nor a shirt that displayed the insignia of many of the armed forces fighting units. Last, a shirt depicting "the quintessential political message the school here is trying to promote – 'Guns and School Don't Mix' – would, under a reasonable interpretation, be prohibited" under the policy (p. 260).

The court concluded that the dress code policy was overbroad because it was "practically limitless" and "excluded a broad range and scope of symbols, images, and political messages that are entirely legitimate and even laudatory" (*Newsom*, p. 260). The circuit court held that the dress policy was unconstitutional as a violation of students' First Amendment rights.

Wrestling with the issue of student expression through clothing and appearance in *Barr* v. *Lafon* (2008), the Sixth Circuit attempted to resolve "how to balance some students' rights to free speech with the rights of other students to be secure and to be left alone" (p. 562). At issue in the case was students' right to wear clothing depicting the Confederate flag. The Blount County School District in Tennessee enacted a ban on wearing clothing displaying the Confederate flag after increased levels of racial tension. Racial tension was illustrated through racial graffiti, threats against black students, fights between white and black students, "hit lists," and threats of bringing guns to school and hanging students. The school district's attempt to quash the tension by enacting the ban did not have an immediate effect. In an eight-month period following the ban, there were 23 violations of the dress code that involved wearing a depiction of the Confederate flag.

Tinker governed the situation because wearing the clothing constituted pure speech that was not lewd or endorsed by the school. Because the Confederate flag clothing was considered pure speech, the court had to determine if the ban was necessary to "avoid material and substantial interference with schoolwork or discipline" (*Barr*, p. 565, internal quotations omitted). The students favoring wearing depictions of the Confederate flag argued that there was no evidence that the students wearing depictions of the Confederate flag actually caused disruption. However, the court pointed out that *Tinker* does not require a disruption to actually occur.

The court expressed that it was only required to determine if the school acted reasonably in *forecasting* substantial disruption. The circumstances revealed that there was substantial evidence of potential disruption because of the racial tension between students and graffiti depicting the confederate flag with a noose. The court concluded that the tension and the symbolism of the Confederate flag "meant that the Confederate flag would likely have a disruptive effect on school" (p. 567). The court explained that the ban was not based on the notion that some students found the Confederate flag offensive but was a constitutional action because of "the disruptive potential of the flag in a school where racial tension is high and serious racially motivated incidents, such as physical altercations or threats of violence, have occurred" (p. 568).[72] Confederate flag clothing continues to cause controversy across the country regardless of the number of cases decided by the courts. In 2009, the Eighth Circuit Court of Appeals and Fifth Circuit Court of Appeals - and the Sixth Circuit Court of Appeals again in 2010 - each addressed high school situations that reflected similar circumstances to those faced by the Sixth Circuit in *Barr* (compare *B.W.A. v. Farmington R-7 Sch. Dist.* (2009), *A.M.* and *McAllum v. Cash* (2009), *DeFoe v. Spiva* (2010) and *Barr*). Like in *Barr*, it was determined that based on the racial tension that existed in the school district it could reasonably forecast that allowing the students to wear such clothing would create a material and substantial disruption of the school (and learning) environment. (*B.W.A.* p. 740; *A.M.*, p. 222, *DeFoe*, p. *10). Just as their sister court did in *Barr*, the Eighth Circuit and Fifth Circuit found that a ban on students wearing clothing depicting the Confederate flag did not violate the students' free speech rights.

The dress code cases consider numerous factors and the discussed decisions represent the different approaches that the courts utilize when addressing dress code free speech/expression claims. Further, the specific circumstances under which a dress code is implemented often play an important role in determining the constitutionality of the dress code. The specific nature of the cases makes it difficult to generalize specific student speech rights regarding dress beyond the fact that the majority of the courts appear to take a firm stance against students wearing the Confederate flag or any clothing that could escalate or support circumstances that create racial tension (*See Barr, B.W.A.* and *A.M.* but *also see Barber*).

Although usually examined in terms of the type of clothing or apparel that students may wear, the courts have also looked at the

---

[72] The court also briefly discussed the view-point neutrality of the enforcement of the ban. However, the court determined that the plaintiffs failed to make a showing that the school had enforced the ban in a discriminatory manner (p. 575). Also the court pointed out that the dress code, as it related to the Confederate flag, would be upheld – regardless of possible viewpoint discrimination - because it met the *Tinker* substantial disruption test.

general constitutionality of student dress codes. In general, the courts have stated that the dress code must have a legitimate interest unrelated to the suppression of student expression and that any restriction on student First Amendment freedom is no more than is necessary to carry-out the district's interest (*see Palmer v. Waxahachie Indep. Sch. Dist.*, 2009, p. 510). The court pointed out that schools could have numerous educational interest for implementing a dress code, including reducing disciplinary infractions, instilling self-confidence and increasing attendance (p. 510). While upholding the specific dress code at issue in *Palmer*, the Fifth Circuit also articulated that dress codes are generally acceptable under the stated constitutional guidelines, do not offend the First Amendment, and that the "determination of where to draw lines on dress code decisions properly rests with the school board rather that with the federal courts (p. 512, *quoting Hazelwood*, p. 266).

Depending on the circumstances and history surrounding the school and the context of the student attire policy, a student might have the right to wear a certain shirt in one district, but the shirt could be prohibited in the neighboring district's schools. The Supreme Court has not addressed student dress codes in terms of First Amendment free speech and expression. Even if the Supreme Court did hear a dress code case, the lower court opinions suggest that the outcome would be fact-specific and possibly fail to provide a general principle beyond those already announced in *Tinker, Fraser, Kuhlmeier,* and *Morse*.

CHAPTER 13.

BF4eva ;) – Student Posting, Texting, and Blogging – LOL...

An emerging area of students' speech and expression rights is students' use of the Internet and its social networking sites, blogs, email, instant messenger, texting and student-created web sites. The Internet is active in students' private, as well as their school, lives. Personal material(s) developed and published at home can be accessed at school, while school-related materials can be reached from home through the "web." A body of case law is quickly developing concerning students' speech and expression rights related to material generated for, posted to, or visited on the Internet.

Avery Doninger, a student at Lewis S. Mills High School in Connecticut, posted a message on a social networking site critical of the school district and high school administration concerning their treatment of a musical festival she planned. Avery's post was characterized as "offensive and inappropriate" because it used vulgar slang to describe the administration,[73] contained false or misleading information about the musical festival, and stated that phone calls to the

---

[73] "Post," or "posting," is a term used to describe the writing of a message or placing of material on a website. Avery's post read as follows: "jamfest is cancelled due to douchebags in central office....basically, because we sent [the original Jamfest email] out, [Superintendent] Paula Schwartz is getting a TON of phone calls and emails and such....however, she got pissed off and decided to just cancel the whole thing all together, anddd [sic] so basically we aren't going to have it at all, but in the slightest chance we do[,] it is going to be after the talent show on may 18<th>" (p. 206).

139

superintendent had "pissed her [the superintendent] off" (*Doninger* v. *Niehoff*, 2007, p. 202). When the posting was discovered by school administrators, they disqualified Avery from running for senior class secretary. Before she created the post, the administration had cautioned Avery about the proper way to raise concerns at school. The disqualification was Avery's only punishment. School officials claimed the posting "failed to display the qualities of civility and citizenship that the school expected of class officers and leaders" (*Doninger*, p. 202).

Avery filed suit in federal court claiming that her First Amendment free expression rights had been violated and sought a preliminary injunction that would have forced the school to remove the current senior class secretary and hold another election in which Avery could participate. The court sided with the school, and an injunction was not issued. The court took two approaches in addressing Avery's claim. First, the court concluded that Avery did not have a First Amendment right to run for a voluntary extracurricular officer position "while engaging in uncivil and offensive communications regarding school administrators" (*Doninger*, p. 216). The court found that the Internet post violated the school's policy on "cooperative conflict resolution" and contained inappropriate and offensive language. The administrators' decision not to let her run was based on the idea that the views expressed in the post were inconsistent with the values of civility and respect embedded in the role of a class officer (p. 215). The court characterized teaching these qualities as a legitimate school objective and, although possibly not the best resolution to the problem, the court found the solution was reasonable and within the administration's discretion.

Second, the court stated that if forced to apply one of the Supreme Court's student speech and expression frameworks, *Fraser* applied rather than *Tinker*. The court admitted that the expression was created off campus, unlike *Fraser*, but that Avery had every intention of the expression being carried on campus. The expression could be considered on-campus rather than off-campus expression because the content related to school issues and it was reasonably foreseeable that students and school officials would view the post. Thus, the court looked at the expression as school-related and offensive. Although under different factual circumstances, (or if the administration had disciplined Avery in a more severe manner), the result might have been different, the court concluded that the actions of the administration in prohibiting Avery from running for a student leadership position were constitutional (*Doninger*, p. 217). The court reasoned that it is highly appropriate for the school "to prohibit the use of vulgar and offensive terms in public discourse" (p. 217, quoting *Fraser*, p. 683).[74]

Aaron Wisniewski was "IMing" with his friends using AOL's Instant Messenger (IM) application on his home computer. As part of the IM program, individuals can develop a personal icon that appears on their friends' screen whenever the friend receives an instant message from the person. The icon can be copied and shared with others by the friend. As his IM icon, Aaron had a small picture of a gun firing a bullet at a person's head with dots representing blood splatter above the head. Below the drawing was the caption "Kill Mr. VanderMolen." Mr. VanderMolen was Aaron's English teacher at Weedsport Middle School in upstate New York (*Wisniewski* v. *Board of Educ. of the Weedsport Central Sch. Dist.*, 2007). Aaron sent the icon to 15 of his school friends, but not to Mr. VanderMolen nor any school official. Aaron did not access the program from school. The icon was available to his friends for three weeks, and one of Aaron's classmates informed Mr. VanderMolen of the icon and brought him a printed copy of it (*Winsiewski*, p. 36).

Mr. VanderMolen forwarded the image to the high school and middle school principals. The principals contacted the police and called Aaron's parents. Aaron acknowledged creating the icon and was suspended for five days. After conducting an administrative hearing, the board of education adopted the hearing officer's recommendation and suspended Aaron for one semester for threatening a teacher and creating an environment that threatened the health, safety, and welfare of others. Aaron filed suit claiming that the icon was not a "true threat" and the expression was protected under the First Amendment (*Wisniewski*, pp. 36-37).

---

[74] Citing *Fraser*, the court distinguished this case from several others that used *Tinker* in examining internet use on the grounds that Avery intended for the expression to infiltrate the school and targeted the treatment of an official school-sponsored activity in which she was involved.

Applying *Tinker*, the court found that "student expression may not be suppressed unless "school officials reasonably conclude that it will materially and substantially disrupt the work and discipline of the school" (*Wisniewski*, p. 38, quoting *Morse*, p. 2626).[75] The court concluded that even if Aaron's icon was viewed as expression under *Tinker*, "It crosses the boundary of protected speech and constitutes student conduct that poses a reasonable foreseeable risk that the icon...would materially and substantially disrupt the work and discipline of the school" (*Wisniewski*, p. 39). For this type of student behavior, "*Tinker* affords no protection against school discipline" (p. 39).

The court also discussed that the fact Aaron created and disseminated the icon from his computer off school grounds did not insulate him from the school's reach and potential discipline. The Second Circuit had previously held that off-campus conduct can create a "foreseeable risk of substantial disruption" inside the school building. it was reasonably foreseeable that the icon, after being distributed to 15 friends many of whom were classmates, would be seen or brought to the school's attention, and the threatening nature of the icon made it reasonably foreseeable that substantial disruption could or would occur in the school (*Wisniewski*, pp. 39-40). "Foreseeability of both communication to school authorities, including the teacher, and the risk of substantial disruption is not only reasonable, but clear" (p. 40). This permitted school discipline regardless of Aaron's intention behind creating the icon (p. 40 citing *Morse*). Aaron did not have a protected

---

[75] Although the federal district court concluded that the icon was a "true threat" lacking First Amendment protection, the Second Circuit, on appeal, determined that addressing the icon as a "true threat" applied the wrong First Amendment standard. Because of the broad authority possessed by schools to sanction student speech and expression, the circuit court concluded that *Tinker* provided the proper guidelines rather than the stricter "true threats" doctrine. This approach by the Second Circuit differed drastically from other courts that had considered threatening student behavior and applied a "true threats" analysis; however, the approaches have render similar results (*See infra S.G..v. Sayerville Board of Educ.*, 2003; *Lovell v. Poway Unified Sch. Dist.*, 1996).

speech right in creating and using the icon and the school's disciplining of Aaron did not violate the First Amendment.

While courts such as *Wisniewski* used *Tinker's* substantial and materially disruption for punishing expression that was created off school grounds, courts have also utilized *Fraser's* lewd and vulgar speech standard depending on what is contained in the blogged, posted, or tweeted expression. Understanding these varied approaches provides educational leaders with additional information to draw on when making determinations regarding student speech and expression in school. Further, it illustrates the intricate nature of the student speech and expression spectrum, and the complications that can occur when student expression situations seems to spill into more than one category.

The cyber cases demonstrate that this is still an unsettled area of student speech and expression rights. Part of the difficulty is that conduct undertaken off school campus can quickly transform into on-campus school conduct because of the wide accessibility of material on the web. Further, questions remain as to whether a school even has the authority to regulate speech that is developed privately at home. Although the court in *Wisniewski* stated that the student's intent behind creating the icon did not matter, other courts have held that a student's intent – especially when the student did not intend for the material to be shared – does play a factor in the extent a school can regulate student speech and expression (*see Lavine* v. *Blaine Sch. Dist.*, 2001, *infra* p. 195; *Doe v. Pulaski County Special Sch Dist.*, 2002, *infra*, p. 200). The broad accessibility of the web and ability to access, copy, and distribute other's information has created additional difficulty when school leaders attempt to determine the balance between student speech and expression on the internet and maintaining order and discipline in school. This places students in a place of uncertainty regarding the rights they have when using the Internet not only at school but also at home or another location off school grounds.

CHAPTER 14.

Free Speech or Free from Potential Harm

In the wake of the Columbine school shooting and other acts of violence at elementary and high schools, there has been a raised level or concern and awareness surrounding potential school violence. This has led to school personnel being proactive in trying to prohibit violence or to defuse volatile situations and districts enacting very strict policy regarding violent behavior. The result has been an increase in litigation concerning the extent of students' First Amendment free speech and expression rights. The circumstances involved in the cases range from physical altercations between students to interpreting creative works that contain violent references.

During a game of cops and robbers on the playground at recess at his New Jersey elementary school, A.G. – a kindergarten student – exclaimed to his friends, "I'm going to shoot you." A classmate not involved in the game heard A.G.'s comments and reported him to a teacher. The teacher reported the incident to the principal, and A.G. was suspended for three days. In the days leading up to A.G.'s conduct, the school had suffered several incidents of students – either seriously or in jest – making comments about inflicting violence on other students, and in each incident, the student received a three-day suspension.[76] A.G.'s father filed an action in federal court on A.G.'s

---

[76] One student told a classmate he was going to shoot the teacher, another student told a friend he would put a gun in his friend's mouth and kill him, and the third told friends that his mom let him bring guns to school.

behalf alleging that the suspension violated A.G.'s First Amendment free speech rights (*S.G.* v. *Sayerville Board of Educ.*, 2003). The family argued that A.G.'s statements were made in the course of a game, that they did not threaten actual harm and did not substantially disrupt school operations or interfere with other's rights. The school argued that prohibiting threatening speech furthered a legitimate pedagogical interest. The court concluded that a First Amendment violation had not occurred in disciplining A.G. because the "Supreme Court has recognized that a balance must be struck between the student's rights and the school's role in fostering what the Court in *Fraser* termed socially appropriate behavior" (*S.G.*, p. 422). The Third Circuit found that after school administrators determined that simulated gun play and threats of violence were unacceptable, "the balance tilts in favor of the school's discretionary decision making" (p. 423). Further, school's ability to control speech at the elementary level is greater than at the high school level, and that the school's prohibition of gunplay was a reasonable decision related to a legitimate pedagogical concern. Thus, A.G.'s suspicion was reasonable and the suppression of his gun related speech did not violate his First Amendment speech and expression rights.

In a case involving a violent poem written by a high school student, the Ninth Circuit balanced a "student's First Amendment right to free expression against school officials' need to provide a safe environment," and addressed the question "against a backdrop of tragic school shootings, occurring both before and after the events at issue" (*Lavine* v. *Blaine Sch. Dist.*, 2001, p. 983). James Lavine drafted the poem "Last Words" at home one evening.[77] James had been absent

---

[77] The final version read: "As each day passed, I watched, love sprout, from the most, unlikely places, wich [sic] reminds, me that, beauty is in the eye's, of the beholder. As I remember, I start to cry, for I, had leared [sic], this to late, and now, I must spend, each day, alone, alone for supper, alone at night, alone at death. Death I feel, crawlling [sic] down, my neck at, every turn, and so, now I know, what I must do. I pulled my gun, from its case, and began to load it. I remember, thinking at least I won't, go alone, as I, jumpped [sic] in, the car, all I could think about, was I would not, go alone. As I walked, hrough [sic] the, now empty halls, I could feel, my hart pounding. As I approached, the

from school the three previous days, but attended school the day after he wrote the poem. He took the poem to school for his English teacher to review even though the poem was not an assignment or for extra credit. Concerned over what she read, the teacher contacted the school counselor and the vice principal. Based on the poem, additional information from school personnel, previous discipline incidents, a turbulent home situation, and prior communications to school officials concerning suicide, the principal decided to "emergency expel" James. As part of an agreement with the district, James met with a psychiatrist and after three visits and missing 17 days of class, he was allowed to return to school (*Lavine*, pp. 984-986). James filed suit in federal court claiming the poem was protected speech and he was unconstitutionally punished for the content of his poem (p. 987).

The circuit court began its analysis by reiterating, "school violence is an unfortunate reality that educators must confront on an all too frequent basis" (*Lavine*, p. 987). The court found that the school must strike a balance between protecting students' safety and respecting those students' constitutional rights. It was determined that James's poem fell into the category of speech governed by *Tinker* and that a *Tinker* analysis required the court to look at the totality of the circumstances. The circumstances showed: (a) the school had a duty to prevent potential violence on campus, (b) the school was aware of previous suicidal ideations by James, (c) James was involved in a domestic dispute with his father, (d) the family was under extreme financial pressure, (e) James had broken up with his girlfriend and was (reportedly) stalking her, (f) James had past discipline problems, (g)

---

classroom door, I drew my gun and, threw open the door, Bang, Bang, Bang-Bang. When it all was over, 28 were, dead, and all I remember, was not felling, any remorce [sic], for I felt, I was, lensing [sic] my soul, I quickly, turned and ran, as the bell rang, all I could here, were screams, screams of friends, screams of co workers, and just plain, screams of shear horror [sic], as the students, found their, slayen [sic] classmates, 2 years have passed, and now I lay, 29 roses, down upon, these stairs, as now, I feel, I may, strike again. No tears, shall be shead [sic], in sarrow [sic], for I am, alone, and now, I hope, I can feel, remorce [sic], for what I did, without a shed, of tears, for no tear, shall fall, from your face, but from mine, as I try, to rest in peace, Bang!" (pp. 983-984).

James had been absent for three days prior to submitting the poem, and (h) The content of his poem, "Last Words." The court acknowledged that individually, a single finding would not have justified the expulsion, but looking at all the factors the court held the circumstances were adequate to lead school leaders to reasonably forecast a substantial and material disruption (p. 990). On the basis of the totality of the circumstances, the court held that the emergency expulsion was reasonable.

The court went on to explain that the poem's content was only one factor in James's expulsion and it was because of the poem that the school's actions were evaluated under the First Amendment. The record clearly demonstrated that several other factors played into the expulsion decision. The school was generally concerned about the students' safety, which the court believed was demonstrated by the immediate action that took place after the poem was submitted to the teacher. James was not disciplined *exclusively* for the specific content of the poem; it was one factor in making the decision that the expulsion for *safety* concerns was reasonable. The court concluded the decision did not violate James's First Amendment rights.

Sarah Lovell threatened her school counselor when meeting with her about changing Sarah's schedule. The guidance counselor claimed that Sarah told her "if you don't give me the schedule change I'm going to shoot you;" however, Sarah stated that she only said "I'm so angry, I could just shoot someone." The guidance counselor sought out the vice principal and told him that she felt threatened by the student's statement and reported that Sarah was angry and emotionally out of control when making the statement. The vice principal met with Sarah, the counselor, and Sarah's parents to discuss the situation. After the meeting, Sarah was suspended for three days. Sarah's parents learned that a discipline report agreeing with the counselor's account of events was placed in Sarah's file, and they filed suit claiming that the suspicion violated Sarah's First Amendment free speech rights (*Lovell v. Poway Unified Sch. Dist.*, 1996).

At the outset of its discussion, the Circuit Court stated that threats are not afforded any First Amendment protection regardless of the forum. Thus, the court did not need to use the Supreme Court's student speech decisions because it did not matter where the statement was uttered, it would not receive constitutional protection if deemed a "true threat" (*Lovell*, p. 371). To determine if a statement was considered a "true threat" and afforded no constitutional protection, courts used an objective test: "whether a reasonable person would foresee that the statement would be interpreted by those to whom the maker communicates the statement as a serious expression of intent to harm of assault" (p. 372).

The court determined that in light of the increasing violence in schools, a reasonable person would have foreseen that the counselor would have taken the comment as a legitimate threat. The court concluded that because a reasonable person would have foreseen that the statement would be interpreted as a threat in the school setting; the statement was not entitled to First Amendment protection and the school did not violate Sarah's right to freedom of speech or expression in suspending her for threatening the school counselor (*Lovell*, p. 373). The court reiterated that the decision was not based on the counselor's fear, but rather on the notion that Sarah (or a person in her position) would have reasonably known that such a statement would be taken seriously.

The Eighth Circuit Court of Appeals also considered a "true threat" situation in *Doe* v. *The Pulaski County Special Sch. Dist.* (2002). During the summer before his eighth grade year, "J.M. drafted two violent, misogynic, and obscenity-laden rants expressing a desire to molest, rape, and murder K.G, his ex-girlfriend" (*Doe*, p. 619). Over the summer, J.M. had several conversations with K.G., told her about the letters, and informed her that they contained statements about killing her. However, J.M. refused to read the letters to K.G. or give them to her. J.M.'s best friend, D.M., found the letters one night while spending the night. He read the letters, but J.M. refused to provide him copies. At K.G.'s prodding D.M. took the letters without J.M.'s permission, transported the letters to school, and gave them to K.M. on the second day of school. K.M. read the letters in her gym class and a classmate immediately reported the threat to the school resource officer. The resource officer visited the gym and found K.M. crying. The officer reported the situation to the school principal. After conducting an investigation that revealed the previously stated facts, the principal recommended that J.M. be expelled for his eight-grade school year for making terroristic threats against K.M. (pp. 619-620).[78] The school board upheld the principal's recommendation and J.M. filed suit in federal court seeking reinstatement and claiming that the expulsion violated his First Amendment free speech rights.

The Eighth Circuit immediately proceeded with a true threats inquiry. The court noted: "Free speech protections do not extend...to certain categories or modes of expression, such as obscenity, defamation, and fighting words" and that the "Supreme Court recognized that threats of violence also fall within the realm of speech that the government can proscribe without offending the First Amendment" (*Doe*, p. 622). The court explained that the government had an "overriding interest" in protecting its citizens from violence or threatened violence. The Eighth Circuit articulated the challenge as determining exactly what constitutes a true threat:

> The federal courts of appeals that have announced a test to parse true threats from protected speech essentially fall into two camps. All the courts to have reached the issue have consistently adopted an objective test that focuses on whether a reasonable person would interpret the purported threat as a serious expression of an intent to cause a present or future harm. The views among the courts diverge, however, in determining from whose viewpoint the statement should be interpreted. Some ask whether a reasonable person standing in the shoes of the speaker would foresee that the recipient would perceive the statement as a threat, whereas others ask how a reasonable person standing in the recipient's shoes would view the alleged threat. Our court is in the camp that views the nature of the alleged threat from the viewpoint of a reasonable recipient. (p. 622)

---

[78] The applicable school rule states, "Students shall not, with the purpose of terrorizing another person, threaten to cause death or serious physical injury or substantial property damage to another person or threaten physical injury to teachers or school employees... Students will be suspended immediately and recommended for expulsion."

Before looking at the actual speech at issue in the case, the Eighth Circuit provided that "a true threat is a statement that a reasonable recipient would have interpreted as a serious expression of an intent to harm or cause injury to another" (p. 624). The court also had to dispose of the issue of how the letters made their way to school and into K.M.'s hands. The court acknowledged that although the speaker did not need to actually intend to carry out the threat for the speech to constitute an unprotected true threat, the speaker must intentionally and knowingly communicate the expression to someone before he can be punished for it (*Doe*, p. 624). The court concluded that J.M. intended to communicate the letters because he told K.M. about the letters on the phone and let D.M. read the letters.

The Court then determined whether a reasonable person would have interpreted the letters as a serious expression to commit harm against another. "There is no question that the contents of the letter itself expressed an intent to harm K.G." (*Doe*, p. 625).[79] The court went on to state that most 13-year-old girls "(and probably most reasonable adults)" would find the letters frightening and fear possible violence if they received J.M.'s letter (p. 625). The fact that J.M. did not deliver the letters did not dissuade the court from concluding that the letters were still threatening. The Eighth Circuit upheld the expulsion. The court concluded that a reasonable person standing in K.G.'s place would have considered the letter a serious expression of potential harm, and determined the letter to be a true threat. (pp. 626-627).

Although reaching the same conclusions regarding the "true threat" student expression that was before each court, the Eighth and Ninth Circuits utilized different standards for determining what constitutes a true threat (*compare Lovell* and *Doe*). The Ninth Circuit stated it used

---

[79] The court based this conclusion on the fact that "The letter exhibited J.M.'s pronounced, contemptuous and depraved hate for K.G. J.M. referred to or described K.G. as a bitch, slut, ass, and a whore over 80 times in only four pages. He used the f-word no fewer than ninety times and spoke frequently in the letter of his wish to sodomize, rape, and kill K.G. The most disturbing aspect of the letter, however, is J.M.'s warning in two passages, expressed in unconditional terms, that K.G. should not go to sleep because he would be lying under her bed waiting to kill her with a knife" (p. 625).

an objective test that evaluated whether a reasonable person standing in the place of the speaker would foresee that the statement would be interpreted by a listener as a serious expression of intent to harm (*Lovell*, p. 372). The Eight Circuit also used an objective standard; however, the Eighth Circuit viewed the situation from the perspective of the listener and evaluated how a reasonable person standing in the position of the message recipient would interpret the communication (*Doe*, p. 622). The two views provide an additional example of how the lower courts can take differing approaches to parallel factual situations but still reach similar conclusions.

David Riehm wrote a fantasy murder suicide essay inspired by the shooting that took place at Columbine High School (*Riehm v. Engelking*, 2008).[80] David was a 17-year-old high school student at Cook County High School in Grand Marais, Minnesota. The essay was authored for his creative writing class and was entitled: "Bowling for Cutchenson." The essay contained a graphic depiction of a student returning to school after being expelled from Ms. Cuntchenson's English class and killing her. Ms. Merdhon, David's teacher, found the essay disturbing and took it as a personal threat. She reported David to the principal. After reading the essay, the principal suspended David. The material was forwarded to the Assistant Cook County Attorney and a "Child Welfare Assessment" case was opened based on the situation. David spent one night in state custody undergoing a psychiatric evaluation because of the threatening nature of the writing and the fear that David may be a danger to himself or others; however, he was released to his mother the next day. In response, David filed suit claiming that the school (and city) violated his First, Fourth, and Fourteenth Amendment rights.

In regard to the First Amendment claim, the Eighth Circuit Court of Appeals reiterated that the First Amendment does not protect speech that is considered a true threat (p. 963). The court described the essay as depicting "an obsession with weapons and gore, a hatred for his [David's] English teacher with a similar name,…a surprise attack at a high school, and the details of his teacher's murder and the narrator's

---

[80] David actually wrote three short essays. All three essays were considered "disturbing;" however, the third essay formed the basis for the litigation.

suicide" (p. 695). The detail created a clear conclusion that the essay was a serious threat to David's English teacher. Thus, it was not protected private expression under *Tinker* and not afforded First Amendment protection.

During a diversity assembly at New Brighton Area High School in Pennsylvania, Cory Johnson was invited on stage to participate in a demonstration conducted by the guest speaker. For the demonstration, the presenter nicknamed each student; Johnson was nicknamed "Osama bin Laden." Johnson did not object at the time and participated in the presentation. The next day students and at least one teacher referred to Johnson as "Osama" or "Osama bin Laden" (*Johnson* v. *New Brighton Area Sch. Dist.*, 2008, p. *2). When a friend approached Johnson in the library and asked, "What's up Osama?" Johnson claimed that he replied in a joking fashion, "If I were Osama, I would already have pulled a Columbine" (p. *3).[81] The librarian heard the exchange. Although she thought Johnson might be joking, she interpreted the comment as a threat and notified administration of the outburst. She did not say anything to Johnson or prohibit him from leaving the library before making the call. In response to the call, the principal met with Johnson. Johnson admitted making the statement and the principal suspended him for 10 days and precluded him from attending his senior prom. The superintendent upheld the suspension because the "Columbine statement constituted a terroristic threat" (p. *6).

Johnson filed suit claiming that the speech was First Amendment free speech protected under *Tinker*. Although the court applied *Tinker*, it found that the evidence revealed that the school "perceived Johnson's speech to be in violation of the core educational mission of the school, and more importantly, led them to be concerned for the safety of all the other school students" (p. *25). The court concluded that the school's actions were not based on a desire to avoid controversy; rather, they were taken because the school officials forecasted "substantial disruption or material interference with school activities would occur" (p. *25).

---

[81] The librarian claimed that students were yelling at Johnson – "Yo, Osama, go to class," and Johnson responded, "If you guys don't quit calling me that, I'm going to pull a Columbine" (p. *3).

The court also noted that Johnson's speech fell "outside the bounds of political speech described in *Tinker*" (p. *26). The reference to Columbine made the speech more of a "true threat" or "fighting words." The court concluded that the term "Columbine, connotes death as a result of one or more students shooting another and school staff," and when uttered at school while a student seems angry, can be reasonably understood by the administration as a true threat (p. *26). Thus, the *Tinker* analysis did not need to be applied because the First Amendment offers no protection to speech that constitutes a "true threat."

While schools and courts clearly take threats and violence in school extremely seriously, not every "threat" results in a proper suspension. There are circumstances where it is clearly not reasonable to believe that a student's actions constituted a true threat of violence:

> B.C. was, at the time of the infraction, a ten-year-old fifth-grade student; his apparent threat was made in crayon in direct response to a school assignment; he did not show the assignment to any classmates but rather handed it directly to his teacher; and B.C. had no other disciplinary history that would suggest a violent tendency. (*Cuff v. Valley Central Sch. Dist.* 2009)

The threat in question was B. C.'s writing "blow up the school with all the teachers in it" in crayon on a school assignment (p. 692). In response to this writing, the school suspended B.C. for six (6) days for making the threat. The court concluded, "based on these facts, that it was [not] reasonable as a matter of law to foresee a material and substantial disruption to the school environment" and that as such the First Amendment does not allow for punishment of the student's speech (p.693).[82]

Violence and threats of violence are legitimate concerns in America's public schools. The courts' decisions demonstrate that

---

[82] *Cuff* was only at the pleadings stage meaning that a trial had not taken place. No additional court opinions – regarding this matter - were available at the time of publication.

school administrators will be granted discretion in maintaining safety in the school building. Although some courts have utilized *Tinker* and *Fraser* in determining the constitutionality of threatening speech and expression, the judicial trend has been treating this type of student expression in school as a true threat, which is afforded no constitutional protection. The courts have provided school leaders with great latitude in suppressing this type of expression because as the Eighth Circuit stated, "the government has an overriding interest in protecting individuals from the fear of violence...and from the possibility that the threatened violence will occur" (*Doe*, p. 622). Schools and the courts have put a premium on keeping students safe, and this duty seems to trump students' First Amendment free speech rights in school.

The Importance of the Lower Court Decision

Although the lower federal court decisions demonstrate that the federal courts usually apply the principles from the Supreme Court's student speech and expression decisions with uniformity, the decisions reveal that the varied circumstances under which the courts must apply the Supreme Court's announced principles can result in diverse conclusions and some divergence about concepts within the principles. The specific facts involved in a student speech or expression situation play a prominent role in the outcome. The lower court decisions display that determining the extent to which school administrators may limit student speech and expression is not as simple as defining or restating the Supreme Court's holdings.

The Supreme Court's decisions do not cover every circumstance. The lower federal courts (and school administrators must) evaluate specific facts in light of the special characteristics of the school environment and apply the Supreme Court's principles to reach constitutional solutions to specific situations. The opinions also reiterate that deference is provided to local school administrators decisions, even when the court does not agree with the wisdom of the decision made by the school officials as long as it does not offend the Constitution (*See DeFabio v. East Hampton Union Free School Dist.*, 2010). The lower federal court decisions are important because they connect specific student speech and expression issues to the principles established by the Supreme Court and demonstrate the complexity of the student speech and expression in school landscape. "It is axiomatic that students do not shed their constitutional rights to freedom of speech or expression at the schoolhouse gate. Despite this well-established principle, school officials nonetheless retain some authority, consistent with fundamental constitutional safeguards, to prescribe and control conduct in the school" (*A.M. ex rel. McAllum v. Cash*, 2009, p.221 *quoting Tinker*, p. 504 (internal quotations omitted)).

PART III

CHAPTER 15

Touring the Student Speech and Expression Legal Landscape

Educators must be knowledgeable of student speech and expression rights in school. They must be comfortable with the awesome responsibility of maintaining a sound educational environment while respecting students' First Amendment speech and expression rights in school. Educators must be confidant in their decisions that affect this delicate balance. Understanding the realm of student speech in specific areas or speech and expression allows educational leaders to make informed decisions regarding student speech and expression rights in school when faced with student speech and expression challenges.

The Supreme Court's Perspective of Student Expression in School

In rendering decisions concerning students' speech and expression rights and corresponding limitations, several constants appear throughout the Supreme Court's decisions. The principles were described by the Supreme Court in *Tinker* v. *Des Moines Indep. Cmty. Sch. Dist.* (1969), *Bethel Sch. Dist.* v. *Fraser* (1986), *Hazelwood School Dist.* v. *Kuhlmeier* (1988), and *Morse* v. *Frederick* (2007). These principles have been utilized and sometimes slightly modifies by the lower federal courts when faced with student speech issues.

First, since *Tinker*, the Court has embraced the conclusion that special circumstances exist in the school environment (*see Tinker*, p. 507). The special circumstances of the school setting mandate that student rights in school may be limited differently and more extensively than constitutional rights outside of school (*Morse*, pp. 2628-2629). Although the Supreme Court has acknowledged that students retain constitutional rights in school, the Court has announced that student rights are not coexistent with those of adults and can be limited in the school setting (*Fraser*, p. 267). As the Supreme Court reiterated in *Morse*, "While children assuredly do not shed their constitutional rights...at the schoolhouse gate...the nature of those rights is what is appropriate for children in school. In particular, the school setting requires some easing of the restrictions," to which school leaders would be subject outside the school context, allowing greater curtailing of student rights in school (pp. 2628-2629).

Second, the Court has specified that the age and maturity level of a student may play a role in the extent of constitutional protection afforded in the school setting (*Fraser*, p. 684; *Hazelwood*, p. 271). The Court has considered not only the age of the child offering the speech or expression but also the age of students that hear or receive the expression (*Fraser*, p. 684). This does not mean that elementary or younger secondary level students do not retain First Amendment speech and expression rights, but the schools' freedom to regulate student rights is greater in the elementary context than at the high school level because of the reduced maturity level of the students.

Third, the Court has reinforced that the primary responsibility for educating students rests with the local school authorities (*Hazelwood*, p. 273). "The education of the Nation's youth is primarily the responsibility of parents, teachers, and state and local school officials, and not of the federal judges" (*Hazelwood*, p. 273). Although the Court is willing to decide the constitutionality of a school rule or the constitutional limits of a student right, the Supreme Court has consistently shown deference for educators' decisions when the decisions related to pedagogical concerns and involved expression offered in the course of a school-sponsored activity or curriculum-related event (*Hazelwood*, p. 272; *Morse*, p. 2625).

Last, the Court has established *Tinker, Fraser, Hazelwood*, and *Morse* as delineating the boundaries of student speech and expression in school (*Morse*, pp. 2625-2626). The Supreme Court summarized its past student expression decisions in *Morse*:

> *Tinker* held that student expression may not be suppressed unless school officials reasonably conclude that it will materially and substantially disrupt the work and discipline of

the school ... [T]he mere desire to avoid the discomfort and unpleasantness that always accompany an unpopular viewpoint, or an urgent wish to avoid the controversy which might result from the expression ... was not enough to justify banning a silent, passive expression of opinion, unaccompanied by any disorder or disturbance. This Court's next student speech case was *Fraser*...[T]he Court also reasoned that school boards have the authority to determine what manner of speech in the classroom or in school assembly is inappropriate ... For present purposes, it is enough to distill from *Fraser* two basic principles. First, *Fraser*'s holding demonstrates that "the constitutional rights of students in public school are not automatically coextensive with the rights of adults in other settings...Second, *Fraser* established that the mode of analysis set forth in *Tinker* is not absolute.
...*Kuhlmeier*, concerned expressive activities that students, parents, and members of the public might reasonably perceive to bear the imprimatur of the school. This Court reversed, holding that "educators do not offend the First Amendment by exercising editorial control over the style and content of student speech in school-sponsored expressive activities so long as their actions are reasonably related to legitimate pedagogical concerns...And, like *Fraser*, it confirms that the rule of *Tinker* is not the only basis for restricting student speech (*Morse*, pp. 2626-2627, internal citations and quotations omitted).

In *Morse*, the Court established an additional limitation for student expression, and it determined that the First Amendment to the U.S. Constitution does not require school officials to tolerate student speech and expression in school or at school events that promotes or endorses illegal drug use or the dangers associated with drug use (*Morse*, 2629).

The Supreme Court's Principles for Addressing Student Speech and Expression in School

The Supreme Court's approach – discussed in the previous section – provides a foundation for addressing student speech and expression in school. Specifically, the Supreme Court has developed four specific principles for addressing student speech and expression issues in school. These principles are outlined in Table 1.

Table 1
Supreme Court Principles for Addressing Student Expression in School

1. School officials may restrict students from participating in speech and expression that materially and substantially disrupts the educational process, the maintaining of discipline, could reasonably be forecasted to disrupt the educational process, or infringes on the rights of other students.	*Tinker*, 1969
2. School officials may suppress or limit student speech and expression that is lewd, uncivil, vulgar, or obscene in the classroom or school activities and may take steps to separate the school from the speech or expression.	*Fraser*, 1986
3. When students participate in school-sponsored or curriculum-related activities, school officials may exert the most control over student speech and expression and limit such expression when based on legitimate pedagogical concerns.	*Hazelwood*, 1988
4. School officials may restrict student speech and expression that promotes or encourages illegal drug use.	*Morse*, 2007

Through its decisions, the Court has announced limitations on student expression in school; the four principles articulated in Table 1. School officials do not have to tolerate speech that materially disrupts the educational process or the learning environment or expression that they reasonably believe could create a substantial disruption in the future. Similarly, school officials may prohibit students from using speech and expression that is lewd, vulgar, or uncivil, or promotes or endorses the use of illegal drugs. Last, school officials may suppress and limit student speech and expression when the student is engaged in a school-sponsored or curriculum-related activity and the limitation is reasonably related to a legitimate pedagogical concern.

The Court has broadly defined curriculum-related activity to include a range of activities and learning experiences that take place outside the classroom. Further, the Court has held that a legitimate pedagogical concern does not have to specifically reflect a portion of the curriculum. These limitations inform school officials that student speech and expression rights are not absolute and provide broad categories of expression that may be curtailed depending of the specific circumstances confronting the school leader.

The Supreme Court discussed student speech and expression in terms of conduct that students should avoid and limitations school administrators may impose. The decisions do not articulate behaviors that students *must* exhibit. Expression that exceeds the announced limits provides school officials with the ability to limit the speech or expression and exposes the student to possible discipline because the speech or expression was not constitutionally protected.

For example, in *Morse* the Supreme Court specifically stated the narrow issue as whether "a principal may, consistent with the First Amendment, restrict student speech at a school event, when that speech is reasonably viewed as promoting illegal drug use" (*Morse*, p. 2625). The Court stated that the "special circumstances of the school environment...allow *schools* to *restrict* student expression" (p. 2629, emphasis added). The reasoning and holding spoke to school administrators' abilities related to constitutionally limiting student expression; it did not speak to an affirmative responsibility on the part of the student. The decision provided a principle for school officials to use in making informed determinations regarding the types of student speech and expression that may be limited. It did not saddle students with an express specific legal responsibility. The decision provided school officials the ability to limit how a student spoke about illegal drug use during a school-sponsored event, if he chose to speak on the topic.

In *Fraser*, the Court spoke of the school's right to limit speech that was lewd and vulgar. The Court spoke in terms of schools having the right to separate themselves from speech and conduct that was "wholly inconsistent with the fundamental values of" the school, and that the school had a responsibility to protect other students from vulgar language (*Fraser*, pp. 681, 683, 686-687). The opinion focused on the appropriate conduct of the school and school administrators in constitutionally limiting student expression.

Forty years ago, the Supreme Court established that students do not shed their First Amendment speech and expression rights when they enter the schoolhouse. Since the Court's recognition of student First Amendment rights, the Court has wrestled with the proper extent of constitutional protection that should be extended to students while in school or on school grounds. The broad freedom of student speech and expression originally granted in *Tinker* is gone. The material and substantial disruption principle remains, but it has been joined by three other student speech and expression principles that have muddied the actual speech and expression freedom *Tinker* was perceived to provide. As Justice Thomas offered in *Morse*, the Court has taken a patchwork approach to defining the extent of students' First Amendment speech and expression rights in school (*Morse*, p. 2636).

The Supreme Court has provided four principles that express the broad limitations of student speech and expression in school. Because of the fact-specific nature of the circumstances in each case, the four Supreme Court decisions concerning student speech and expression do not specifically or overtly address every possible speech and expression situation that a school administrator could potentially face. The principles provide school officials direction with regard to the type of expression that may be limited; however, the principles, in abstract form, provide educators with limited guidance on how they might be applied to a particular factual situation beyond those already specifically addressed by the Supreme Court. The lower federal court decisions regarding student speech and expression in school provide a more specific framework for how the Supreme Court principles can be applied in varied circumstances and a more complete picture of the student speech and expression landscape.

Further Defining the Limitations of Student Speech and Expression

The lower federal courts have utilized the Supreme Court student speech and expression principles, expressed in Table 1, for evaluating the constitutionality of school authorities' decisions regarding student speech and expression in a variety of specific circumstances. In doing so, the lower courts have addressed factual situations that were different from those encountered by the Supreme Court in its original decisions. They have also reviewed factual situations similar to the facts confronted by the Supreme Court in *Tinker, Fraser, Kuhlmeier,* and *Morse,* but in certain situations they have used variations of the student expression principles originally utilized by the Court to reach conclusion.

The lower federal courts consistently return to the four Supreme Court principles when making decision regarding the constitutionality of student speech and expression or school officials' imposed limitations. The lower federal courts' interpretations (and application) of the Supreme Court principles reiterate that the four Supreme Court principles provide the basis for any decision school officials should make when limiting student speech and expression in school, as well as provide rationale for why certain student expression is constitutionally protected. The individual decisions showcase the spectrum of speech and expression situations that can be covered by the principles, provide examples of circumstances school administrators might confront in the future, and explain how each situation relates back to one (or more) of the four Supreme Court principles contained in Table 1.

The lower federal court decisions provide information to fill in gaps between the broad Supreme Court principles and assist in bringing detail to the spectrum of student speech and expression rights in school under the First Amendment to the U.S. Constitution. The decisions track the changes in the Supreme Court's position on the proper extent of student speech and expression rights in school. The decisions showcase the flexibility and wide applicability of the principles and reveal how the principles overlap and intersect. They reinforce the idea that more than one principle might be applicable to a given set of facts, and provide innovative rationale for supporting students' right or a school leader's proposed limitations.

The lower court decisions take the Supreme Court principles out of a vacuum and apply the abstract principles – "material and substantial disruption," "school-sponsored or curricular related activity," and "legitimate pedagogical concern" – to practical use. Like the Supreme Court decisions, the lower federal court decisions cannot cover or address every possible circumstance an educator might face. However, they do provide additional direction for interpreting a situation and determining how to apply the appropriate Supreme Court principle to specific facts where the constitutionality of student speech or expression is at issue.

By identifying and reviewing the current legal boundaries of student speech and expression rights in school, as developed and defined by the U.S. federal courts, educators are better equipped to make informed decisions in limiting student expression when confronted with such situations. The lower federal courts have addressed a wide array of circumstances that have been encountered by school administrators. The decisions assist in identifying the current boundaries surrounding student speech and expression in school, illustrate the complex nature of the student speech and expression rights spectrum, and highlight the challenges associated with making informed decisions regarding student speech and expression under the First Amendment to the U.S. Constitution.

While the courts have stated that educational decisions should be left to local school boards and school administrators, having a better understanding of the courts' view(s) provides educators with guidance as to how a specific student speech and expression circumstance aligns with one (or more) of the four Supreme Court principles and whether the decision is more than likely constitutional. School leaders can learn from past circumstances and decisions and use this knowledge as a tool when making informed decisions concerning whether student speech or expression, or a potential limitation on the speech or expression, is legal and constitutional. For educational leaders' purposes, it brings clarity to the legal quagmire that surrounds student speech and expression in school.

The constitutional boundaries of student speech and expression rights in school are identified by applying the Supreme Court's student speech and expression principles to specific factual situations encountered by school leaders and addressed by the federal courts. As the Supreme Court has stated, while students do not "shed their constitutional rights...at the schoolhouse gates...the nature of those rights is what is appropriate for children in school" (*Morse*, p. 2627, quoting *Tinker*, pp. 506 and citing *Acton*, pp. 655-656). Table 1 identifies the Supreme Court student speech and expression principles and the lower court decisions exemplify how the speech and expression principles may be applied to a specific set of facts. These conclusions add depth to the student speech and expression landscape by identifying specific speech and expression situations and providing detail about the federal courts' approach(es) to student speech and expression issues that do not necessarily reflect the exact factual situations faced by the Supreme Court in *Tinker, Fraser, Kuhlmeier*, or *Morse*.

Connection to other Student Constitutional Rights

The First Amendment to the U.S. Constitution provides:

> Congress shall make no law respecting an establishment of religion, or prohibiting the free exercise there of; or abridging the freedom of speech, or of the press; or the right of the people peaceably to assemble, and to petition the Government for a redress of grievances. (*Wallace* v. *Jaffree*, 1985, p. 39)

Although distinct bodies of jurisprudence have developed around specific individual student rights that the Court has announced exist under the Constitution, the Supreme Court has utilized reasoning and conclusions developed in one area of student rights – such as student search under the Fourth Amendment - to support and bolster decisions in other areas of student rights and responsibility such as speech under the First Amendment (*see e.g. Morse* v. *Frederick*, 2007, p. 2628 applying principles developed in *New Jersey v. T.L.O.* (1985) and *Brd. of Edu. of Indep. Sch. Dist. No. 94 of Pottawatomie County* v. *Earls* (2002)). By analyzing the specific conclusions in one area, general principles applied in all areas of student rights and responsibilities can become more visible. These concepts transcend nearly all student rights and responsibilities under the Amendments to the Constitution (*see generally T.L.O.*).

The cross-over and applicability of the courts' decisions in one area of student rights and responsibility to another area of student rights and responsibility is most obvious in the Supreme Court's decisions. As was discussed previously, the Supreme Court often looks to precedent it has set in one area of student rights to support a position it takes in a different student rights context. For example, the Supreme Court in *Morse* turned to the student privacy opinions in *Vernonia Sch. Dist. 47j v. Acton* (1995), and *Board of Education of Independent School District No. 92 of Pottawatomie County v. Earls* (2002), for the proposition that prohibiting student drug use is a substantial and material educational interest (*Morse*, p. 2629). The Court also referenced *Acton* for the limited nature of students' rights in school: "Fourth Amendment rights, no less than First and Fourteenth Amendment rights are different in public schools" (p. 2627, quoting *Acton*, p. 656).

The Supreme Court has clearly utilized rationale established in one area of student rights in analyzing other student rights issues. The Supreme Court in *T.L.O.* spoke about the special circumstances in the school building (*T.L.O.*, p. 340, 348) and the Court in *Hazelwood* referenced *T.L.O.* for this point (*Hazelwood*, p. 266). Furthermore, *Morse* relied heavily on the Supreme Court's development of the legitimate pedagogical interest of prohibiting student illegal drug use in *Acton* and *Earls* for its *Morse's* holding (*Morse*, p. 2629).

The Supreme Court decisions regarding religion have pointed to the need to not infringe on other students' rights as well as the impressionable nature of students at certain ages (*Lee*, p. 592; *Santa Fe Sch. Dist v. Doe*, 2000, p. 311 – 312; *Mergens*, p. 250). The lower courts in the speech and expression context have also embraced these principles (*i.e. Walz*, p. 276). In addition, the Supreme Court has utilized its school forum analysis developed in *Hazelwood* in its religious expression in schools decisions (*see Doe*, p. 302 – 303 applying *Hazelwood*). Granted, every circumstance is unique and cross-over not always visible, but there is usually great consistency in determining if a school's actions violate a student's rights as the Supreme Court has utilized these factors in multiple student rights areas (*See generally Morse, T.L.O., Lee*, and *Doe*).

Although not necessarily by analogy, the Supreme Court speech and expression cases provide five general principles that can be applied to all areas of student rights and responsibilities:

1. Special circumstances exist in schools that make the analysis of student's constitutional rights and responsibilities different than in other context.
2. Differences exist between students at the elementary and secondary level. The maturity level of elementary school students dictates that school administrators be given greater leeway in addressing situations concerning students' constitutional rights because of the increase need to prevent undue influence or coercion and combat the increased impressionability of elementary school children.
3. The school's need to maintain discipline and order in the school environment, to prevent materially and substantial disruption of the education process, and the school's interest in carrying out its legitimate pedagogical concerns will influence decisions concerning students' rights and responsibilities.
4. Whether the school's action was reasonable under the circumstances and related to a legitimate pedagogical interest.
5. A certain amount of deference is afforded school officials' decisions because the main responsibility for the education of the nation's children rests with the local school officials not the nation's courts even if the court does not agree with the wisdom of the school administrator's decision.

These five broad principles have applicability across all areas of student rights and responsibilities because regardless of the specific "right" at issue, the factors and circumstance will be present in school or considered by the court as demonstrated by the Supreme Court's past student rights decisions.

The lower courts have also utilized Supreme Court precedent from other areas for student speech and expression analysis. In Chapter XI: The Student Athlete and Free Speech, the application of the Supreme Court's student privacy rights decisions is discussed in the context of student athletes' speech rights in the Sixth Circuit's decision in *Lowery et. al.* v. *Euverard et. al.* (2007). In determining that student athletes have reduced speech and expression rights, the Sixth Circuit looked to the Supreme Court's holding in *Acton* and *Earls* as support because the Court had already established that student athletes have limited privacy rights. The Sixth Circuit used the rationale employed by the Supreme Court in the privacy context to support its conclusion of reduced rights for student athletes in the speech and expression realm.

Examination of religious rights coupled with (and sometimes required for) free speech analysis is also clearly present in the courts' opinions, as students often allege Free Exercise claims along with free speech and expression claims (*See Curry*, p. 576, 579 – 580; *DeNooyer v. Livonia Public Sch. Dist.*, 1992, p. 753; *Bannon v. Sch. Dist. of Palm Beach*, 2004, p. 1220) The lower courts have applied a number of the above factors when reaching conclusions on issues outside the free speech claim. Again, reiterating that cross-over is often present in the courts' analysis. A court may not be able to apply all of the factors and all five may not even be present given the specific circumstances facing the court; however, the concepts imbedded in the factors do have value in numerous student rights areas.

Constant Evolution

Teacher and administrator's roles are continually changing in response to students' actions, regardless if the student action is sanctioned by the Court or protected by the Constitution. The changing role of the school official depends heavily on whether the student right is expanded or limited; however, in either circumstance the role seems to become more challenging. In circumstances where a student right is protected or expanded, the school administration has to work harder to carry out the educational mission of the school and to maintain order and discipline while not infringing on the newly protected right and still ensuring the rights of other students are not infringed.

When *Tinker* was announced, school officials' roles were clearly changed with the mandate that students' retain speech and expression rights in school. Nothing in the cases since *Tinker* suggests that teacher and administrators' roles do not continue to evolve as students' rights and responsibilities do the same. For example In *Barber* v. *Dearborn Pub. Sch.* (2003), the school officials had to allow a student to continue to wear his t-shirt that expressed his political opinion of President

Bush's foreign policy. At the same time, the school needed to continue to promote its pedagogical concerns of diversity and tolerance in a school that had a student population that was approximately one-third students of Middle Eastern descent. This dynamic presented an increased challenge, because the teachers and administrators needed to balance the tolerance of political ideology with the promotion of diversity even when the political ideology being expressed could have been considered culturally insensitive.

If a student right is limited, this does not necessarily reduce the challenge associated with enforcing the limitation. For example in situations concerning the distribution of religious tracts at the elementary level, school officials have to balance the rights of the student who wants to distribute literature against the rights of students (and parents) who believe such distribution is endorsed by the school. Even if the distribution right is limited such as in *Harlerr v. Darr* (1996), the school still allowed limited distribution but had to separate itself from the message of the distribution adding to the educational leaders challenge.

While the Supreme Court's student speech and expression decisions provide direction for school leaders and the lower federal courts application of these principles add clarity to the student speech and expression spectrum, the student speech and expression landscape remains muddled. As Justice Thomas has stated, the student speech and expression framework represents a patchwork approach to addressing these student rights in school. The landscape continues to evolve and morph as students engage in new and different types of speech and expression and school leaders attempt to limit the expression under the First Amendment.

Educational leaders are charged with the massive responsibility of educating the nation's students and maintaining a positive educational environment. Teachers, school administrators, and district leaders must be aware of the legal and constitutional limits that surround student speech and expression in school and what should be considered when making determinations regarding student speech and expression issue. This understanding is crucial to maintaining a productive educational environment as the constitutional rights of students cannot be trampled in an attempt to carry out school leaders' educational goals.

References

Abdul-Muhammad v. Kempker, 450 F.3d 350 (8th Cir. 2006).

Abrams, J. Marc and S. Mark Goodman (1988). End of an Era? The Decline of Student Press Rights in the Wake of Hazelwood School District v. Hazelwood. Duke Law Journal, 1988 Duke L.J. 706.

ARK. CODE ANN. §§6-18-1201 to -1204 (2008).

A.M. ex rel. McAllum v. Cash, 585 F.3d 214 (2009).

B.W.A. v. Farmington R-7 Sch. Dist., 554 F.3d 734 (2009).

Bannon v. Sch. Dist. of Palm Beach County, 387 F.3d 1208 (11th Cir. 2004).

Barber v. Dearborn Pub. Sch., 286 F. Supp. 2d 847 (E.D. Mich. 2003).

Barr v. Lafon, 553 F.3d 463 (6th Cir. 2008).

Bell et al. v. U-32 Brd. of Edu. et al., 630 F. Supp. 939 (D. VT 1986).

Best, John W. And Kahn, James V. (1998). *Research in Education*. Needham, MA: Allyn & Bacon.

Bethel Sch. Dist. v. Fraser, 478 U.S. 675 (1986).

Black's Law Dictionary (8th ed. 2004).

Board of Education of Independent School District No. 92 of Pottawatomie County v. Earls, 536 U.S. 822 (2002).

Board of Education, Island Trees Union Free School District No. 26 v. Pico, 457 U.S. 853 (1982).

Boggs, Teresa J. (2005). The First Amendment Rights of High School Students and Their Student Newspapers. MA Thesis, West Virginia University, United States – West Virginia.

Borger v. Kenosha Unified Sch. Dist. No. 1, 888 F. Supp. 97 (E.D. Wisc 1995).

Boroff v. Van Wert City Brd. of Edu., 220 F.3d 465 (6th Cir. 2000).

171

Brody v. Spang, 957 F.2d 1108 (3rd Cir. 1992).

Brundage, Anthony (2002). *Going to the Sources*. Wheeling, Il: Harlan Davidson, Inc.

Burch et al. v. Barker et al., 861 F.2d 1149 (9th Cir. 1988).

Busch v. Marple Newtown Sch. Dist., 567 F.3d 89 (3rd Cir. 2009).

Bush v. Dassel-Cokato Bd. of Educ., 745 F. Supp. 562 (D. Minn 1990).

Buss, William G. (1989). School Newspapers, Public Forum, and the First Amendment. Iowa Law Review. 74 Iowa L. Rev. 505.

Bystrom v. Fridley High School, 822 F.2d 747 (8th Cir. 1987).

CAL. EDUC. CODE § 48907 (2008).

Canter, Andrew and Pardo, Gabriel (2008). The Court's Missed Opportunity in Harper v. Poway. Brigham Young University Education and Law Journal. 2008 BYU Educ. & L. J. 125.

Caudillo v. Lubbock Indep. Sch. Dist., 311 F. Supp. 2d 550 (N.D. TX 2004).

Chandler v. McMinnville Sch. Dist., 978 F.2d 524 (9th Cir. 1992).

Child Evangelism Fellowship of Md., Inc. v. Montgomery County Pub. Schs, 373 F.3d 589, 593 (4th Cir. 2004).

Circle Sch. v. Pappert, 381 F.3d 172 (3rd Cir. 2004).

COLO. REV. STAT. § 22-1-120 (2008).

Constitution of the United States of America, Amendment 1. United States Code Services (2008). Matthew Bender & Company, Inc.

Corder v. Lewis Palmer Sch. Dist., 568 F. Supp. 2d 1237 (D. CO 2008).

Corder v. Lewis Palmer Sch. Dist., 566 F.3d 1219 (10th Cir. 2009).

Corales v. Bennett, 567 F.3d 554 (9th Cir. 2009).

Crosby v. Holsinger, 816 F.2d 162 (4th Cir. 1987).

Cuff v. Valley Central Sch. Dist., 341 Fed.Appx. 692 (2nd Cir. 2009).

Curry v. Saginaw City Sch. Dist., 513 F.3d 570 (6th Cir. 2008).

DeFabio v. East Hampton Union Free School Dist., 623 F.3d 71 (2nd Cir. 2010).

DeFoe v. Spiva, 2010 WL 4643256 (6th Cir. 2010).

Dennis v. United States, 341 U.S. 494 (1951).

DeNooyer et al. v. *Livonia Public Sch.*, 1993 U.S. App. Lexis 30084 (6th Cir. 1993).

Desilets ex rel. Desilets v. Clearview Reg'l Bd. of Educ., 137 N.J. 585 (D.N.J. 1994).

Dever, James C (1985). Tinker Revisited: Fraser v. Bethel School District and Regulation of Speech in the Public Schools. 1985 Duke L. J. 1164.

Doe v. *The Pulaski County Special Sch. Dist*, 306 F.3d 616 (8th Cir. 2002).

Doninger v. *Niehoff*, 514 F. Supp. 2d 199 (D. Conn 2007).

Elk Grove Unified Sch. Dist. v. *Newdow*, 542 U.S. 1 (2004).

Faaborg, K (1985). High School Play Censorship: Are Students' First Amendment Rights Violated when Officials Cancel Theatrical Production? Journal of Law and Education. 14 J.L.& Educ. 575.

F.C.C. v. Pacifica Foundation, 438 U.S. 726 (1978).

Flagship Marine Servs. v. Belcher Towing Co., 23 F.3d 341 (11th Cir. 1994).

Fleming v. Jefferson County Sch. Dist. R-1, 298 F.3d 918 (10th Cir. 2002).

Frazier v. Alexandre, 434 F. Supp. 2d 1350 (S.D. FL 2006).

Frazier v. Winn, 535 F.3d 1279 (11th Cir. 2008).

Freeman, Brian A. (1984). Supreme Court and First Amendment Rights of Students in the Public School Classroom: A Proposed Model of Analysis, The; Freeman, Brian A. 12 Hastings Const. L.Q. 1.

Gall, Meredith D, Borg, Walter R. And Gall, Joyce P. (1996). Educational Research An Introduction. 6th Edition. White Plains, NY: Longman Publishers.

Gillman v. Sch. Brd. for Holmes County, 567 F. Supp. 2d 1359 (N.D. FL 2008).

Goodman, Robert S. And Kruger, Evonne Jonas (1988). Data Dredging or Legitimate Research Method? Historiography and Its Potential for Management Research. Academy of Management Review. 13(2), pp. 315-325.

Hafen Bruce C. And Hafen, Jonathan O. (1995). Twenty-five Years after Tinker: Balancing Students' Rights: The Hazelwood Progeny: Autonomy and Student Expression in the 1990's. St. John's Law Review. 69 St. John's L. Rev. 379.

Hansen v. Martin, 293 F. Supp. 2d 780 (E.D. Mich 2003).

Harless v. Darr, 937 F. Supp. 1339 (S.D. IN Feb 1996).

Harper v. Poway Unified Sch. Dist., 127 S. Ct. 1484 (2007).

Harper v. Poway Unified Sch. Dist., 445 F. 3d 1166 (9th Cir. 2006).

Hazelwood School Dist. v. Kuhlmeier, 484 U.S. 260 (1988).

Heinkel v. Sch. Brd., 194 Fed. Appx. 604 (11th Cir. 2006).

Henerey v. City of St. Charles, School District et. al., 200 F.3d 1128 (8th Cir. 1999).

Holloman v. Harland, 116 Fed. Appx. 254 (11th Cir. 2008).

Howell, Martha and Prevenier, Walter (2001). From Reliable Sources: An Introduction to Historical Methods. Ithaca, New York: Cornell University Press.

IOWA CODE § 280.22 (2007).

Johnson v. New Brighton Area Sch. Dist., 2008 U.S. Dist. LEXIS 72023 (W.D. PA 2008).

KAN. STAT. ANN. § 72-1504 to -1506 (2008).

Kuhlmeier v. Hazelwood Sch. Dist, 795 F.2d 1368 (8th Cir. 1987).

Kuhlmeier v. Hazelwood Sch. Dist., 607 F. Supp 1450 (E.D. MO 1985).

Lane, Robert Wheeler (1992). Beyond the schoolhouse gate: Free speech and the inculcation of values. Ph.D. dissertation, The University of Wisconsin - Madison, United States -- Wisconsin. Retrieved April 2, 2009, from Dissertations & Theses @ CIC Institutions database. (Publication No. AAT 9230167).

Lavine v. Blaine Sch. Dist., 257 F.3d 981 (9th Cir. 2001).

Lovell v. Poway Unified Sch. Dist., 90 F.3d 367 (9th Cir. 1996).

Lowery et. Al. v. Euverard et. Al., 497 F.3d 584 (6th Cir. 2007).

M.A.L. v. Stephen Kinsland, 543 F.3d 841 (6th Cir. 2008).

Marshall, Catherine and Rossman, Gretchen B (2006). Designing Qualitative Research. Fourth Edition. Thousand Oaks, CA: Sage Publications.

McCann v. Fort Zumwalt Sch. Dist, 50 F. Supp. 2d 918 (E.D. MO 1999).

McCarthy, Martha M. (1998). The Principal and Student Expression: From Armbands to Tattoos. NASSP Bulletin. 82(599), pp. 18-25.

McCarthy, Martha M (2007). Student Expression Rights: Is a New Standard on the Horizon? 216 Ed. Law. Rep. 15.

MASS. GEN. LAWS ANN. ch. 71, §82 (2008).

Morgan v. Plano Indep. Sch. Dist., 589 F.3d 740 (2009).

Morse v. Frederick, 127 S. Ct. 2618 (2007).

Nairn, Joanna (2008). Free Speech 4 Students? Morse v. Frederick and the Inculcation of Values in Schools. Harvard Civil Rights-Civil Liberties Law Review. 43 Harv. C.R.-C.L. L. Rev. 239.

New Jersey v. T.L.O., 469 U.S. 325 (1985).

Newsom v. Albermarle County Sch. Brd, 354 F.3d 249 (4th Cir. 2003).

Nurre v. Whitehead, 580 F.3d 1087 (9th Cir. 2009).

Nuxoll v. Indian Praire Sch. Dist. #204, 2008 U.S. App. Lexis 8737 (7th Cir. 2008).

Palmer v. Waxahachie Indep. Sch. Dist., 579 F.3d 502 (2009).

Patterson v. McLean Credit Union, 491 U.S. 164 (1989).

Payne v. Tenn., 501 U.S. 808 (1991).

Phillips v. Oxford Separate Municipal Sch. Dist., 314 F. Supp. 2d 643 (N.D. Miss 2003).

Pinard et al v. Clatskanie Sch. Dist 6J, 467 F.3d 755 (9th Cir. 2006).

Planned Parenthood of S. Nev. v. Clark, 941 F.2d 817, 830 (9th Cir. 1991).

Poling v. Ellis Murphy, 872 F.2d 757 (6th Cir. 1989).

Prince v. Massachusetts, 321 U.S. 158 (1944).

Pyle v. The South Hadley Sch. Committee, 824 F. Supp. 7 (D. Mass 1993).

Rabideau v. Beekmantown, 89 F. Supp. 2d 263 (N.D.N.Y. 2000).

Riehm v. Engelking, 538 F.3d 952 (8th Cir. 2008).

S.G. v. Sayreville Brd. of Edu., 333 F.3d 417 (3rd Cir. 2003).

Settle v. Dickson County Sch. Brd., 53 F.3d 152 (6th Cir. 1995).

Slaff, Sara (1987). Silencing Student Speech: Bethel School District No. 403 v. Fraser. American University Law Review. 37 Am. U.L. Rev. 203.

Slotterback v. Interboro School Dist., 766 F. Supp. 280 (D.Pa 1991).

Smith v. Mount Pleasant Public Sch., 285 F. Supp. 2d 987 (E.D. Mich 2003).

Sonkowsky v. Brd of Edu. for Independent Sch. Dist No. 721 et. Al., 2002 U.S. Dist. Lexis 6197 (D.Minn. 2002).

Sosa v. Alvarez-Machain, 542 U.S. 692 (2004).

Spence v. Washington, 418 U.S. 405 (1974).

Steirer et al. v. Bethlehem Area Sch. Dist., 789 F. Supp. 1337 (E.D. Penn 1992).

Tech Law Journal (2008). http://www.techlawjournal.com/glossary/legal/amicus.htm.

Tenet v. Doe, 544 U.S. 1 (2005).

Theodore, George Mitchell (1997). An analysis of selected federal court decisions regarding students' First Amendment rights of expression and speech: Principles for principals. Ph.D. dissertation, The University of Alabama at Birmingham, United States -- Alabama. Retrieved April 2, 2009, from Dissertations & Theses: A&I database. (Publication No. AAT 9818851).

Thibodeaux, Therese. (1987). Bethel School District No. 403 v. Fraser: The Supreme Court Supports School in Sanctioning Student for Sexual Innuendo in Speech. 33 Loy. L. Rev. 516.

Tinker v. Des Moines Indep. Cmty. Sch. Dist., 393 U.S. 503 (1969).

Vernonia Sch. Dist. 47j v. Acton, 515 U.S. 646 (1995).

Virgil v. School Bd., 862 F.2d 1517 (11th Cir. 1989).

Waldman, Emily G. (2008). A Post-Morse Framework for Students' Potentially Hurtful Speech (Religious ands Otherwise). 37 J.L. & Educ. 463.

Wallace v. Jaffree, 472 U.S. 38 (1985).

Walz v. *Egg Harbor Township Brd. of Edu.*, 342 F. 3d 271 (3rd Cir. 2003).

West v. Derby Unified Sch. Dist. No 260, 206 F.3d 1358 (10th Cir. 2000).

West Virginia v. Barnette, 319 U.S. 624 (1943).

Wildman v. Marshalltown, 249 F.3d 768 (8th Cir. 2001).

Wisniewski v. Brd. of Edu. of the Weedsport Central Sch. Dist, 494 F.3d 34 (2007).

Zollo, Nina. (1987). Constitutional Law: School Has Broad Discretion to Prohibit Offensive Student Speech. 39 U. Fla. L. Rev. 193.

Index

CPSIA information can be obtained at www.ICGtesting.com
Printed in the USA
BVOW030413110713

325118BV00003B/7/P